POWERHOUSE OF SUCCESS: MASTER YOUR DAILY HABITS

ANINDITA SAHA

I had no idea that my daily morning journaling would lead to a whole book. Each day, I diligently followed the practices I had written out, and to my surprise, the science behind them were true. Though results may vary from one individual to the next, by regularly applying these tactics, my productivity and well-being transformed.

"Your journey, is meant to be walked, on your terms.

Make mistakes, then learn, then grow, then trust your gut.

If you follow anyone else's advice (without asking what works for you), Your path is not yours anymore — it's theirs.

Stick to your vision and never let anybody else steer your life for you."

NOTE: I've left some **BLANK** pages for you to **WRITE** your thoughts, now as you go through this book, I hope you will fill the rest of the blank pages of your life into the most beautiful ones and add the page numbers, helping to compelete all 156 pages. Stay engaged with me as much as possible!

Contents

Contents

Contents

Start Your Journey With Simple Yet Powerful Habits:

Foreword

Powerhouse of Success: Master Your Daily Habits isn't just another self-help book. It's a guide to transforming your life, not by making massive, overwhelming changes, but by refining the habits that define who you are. This book takes you beyond motivation and into real, actionable strategies that will help you rewire your daily routines for success. As you turn these pages, you'll uncover the science behind habits, learn powerful techniques to build discipline, and discover how tiny improvements can lead to massive, long-term results. Whether you're striving for personal growth, career advancement, or simply a better version of yourself, this book will give you the roadmap to get there.

Preface

This book was born out of my own journey of self-improvement, along with countless stories of successful individuals who mastered their daily habits. I have seen firsthand how small changes, repeated consistently, create massive transformations. Yet, most people struggle to build good habits and break bad ones, not because they lack motivation, but because they don't have the right system in place. That's why I wrote Powerhouse of Success: Master Your Daily Habits. This book is designed to be a practical, no-fluff guide to help you understand the science of habit formation, develop powerful routines, and unlock the potential hidden in your everyday actions.

Acknowledgements

I am beyond grateful to the people who stood by me through this journey. To my parents -your love, support, and belief in me have been my biggest strength. Every step of the way, you reminded me that I am capable, and for that, I am forever thankful. To my dear friend- you were always there to lift me up, encourage me, and push me forward when I doubted myself. Your support meant more than words can express. This book is not just mine; it's a reflection of the love and strength you all gave me. Thank you from the bottom of my heart.

Prologue

Have you ever wondered why some people seem to accomplish so much while others struggle to make progress? Why do some individuals thrive in their careers, maintain their health, and build meaningful relationships—while others feel stuck in the same cycle, year after year? Most people believe success is about intelligence, luck, or having the right opportunities. Think about it: Every successful person you admire, every great achievement in history, was not the result of a single moment, but rather the compounded effect of daily actions. I know this because I've lived it. I've seen how small, daily improvements have transformed not only my own life but also the lives of many around me. I've also experienced the frustration of inconsistency—starting strong but falling back into old patterns. If you've ever felt stuck, unmotivated, or like success is just out of reach, you're not alone. The problem isn't you. The problem is the way we approach success.

This book is here to change that.

Introduction

In this fast-paced generation, productivity is explored as if it's a life-threatening situation. Productivity isn't simply about having additional activities accomplished; it's about growing the right results that instantly would match our personal and occupational realms. It's important to realise that the link between our day-to-day lifestyle choices and our success is very profound. It can be even more small, planned changes in our patterns that can make significant improvements in our productivity and wellness.

Why Productivity Matters

Productivity matters since it provides insight into our capacity or our undiscovered potential that is the cornerstone of success, enabling us to complete assignments efficiently and successfully. Achievement more done is important because it helps us accomplish our goals and relieves some of the pressure of making time for things we want to do more.

The Link Between Lifestyle & Success

Our daily habits and practices directly affect our productivity levels. Regular physical activity, a balanced diet, satisfactory sleep, and stress managing are lifestyle components that really play a major part in fetching out the best in a person. By approving healthy lifestyle, it helps us to get mentally sharp and energetic and enhances our efficacy as a whole.

Small Changes, Big Results

Very little change in our habits can bring considerable improvements in productivity. Setting up a morning routine to do first. Simple action like one of these, many people will agree to starting out with prioritizing tasks and carrying out regular pauses helps in retaining maximum focus and efficiency. These tiny changes, when made regularly, add up over time to major positive results.

How to Use This Book Effectively

Using the book provides the reader with easy-to-follow action plans and ideas for boosting productivity through mindfulness by making sustainable life change. Every chapter comprises steps to take, examples to learn from, recommended exercises for applying these changes effectively. Reading and working on the tips in this book will most certainly put you on a life-transforming journey to increased productivity and success.

Understanding Productivity

CHAPTER ONE

THE SCIENCE BEHIND PRODUCTIVITY

The Role of Habits in Success

Success is not an accident; it is the outcome of frequent actions that align with our clear vision. While our talent and ambition set the stage, it is the habits we cultivate daily that determine whether we reach our goals or fall short. The most successful individuals in any field know that brilliance is built on consistency rather than occasional bursts of effort. Habits shape our mindset, discipline our actions, and create energy that drives long-term achievement.

Every great leader, athlete, entrepreneur, or innovator has relied on structured habits to sharpen their skills and improve their processes. It is not the single revolutionary idea but the disciplined execution of small, productive routines that leads to justifiable success. When we look at high achievers, we often admire their results, yet behind the scenes, their daily habits hold the top-secret to their accomplishments.

Good habits create productivity, reduce decision exhaustion, and systematize success-oriented behaviours. They remove dependence on short-lived motivation and replace it with a system that strengthens discipline and progress. The difference between those who succeed and those who stagnate often lies in the ability to develop, maintain, and refine the right habits over time.

Contrarywise, poor habits can be just as powerful in the opposite direction, leading to 'procrastination', 'self-doubt', and 'wasted potential'. Success, therefore, is not solely about working harder but about working smarter—designing a life where beneficial habits become second nature. The key is to cultivate routines that align with your vision and purpose, ensuring that each day brings you closer to your aspirations.

The role of habits in success is undeniable. Whether it's waking up early, practicing gratitude, setting clear goals, or maintaining a growth mindset, the accumulation of these small actions creates a powerhouse of productivity. Success is not found in a single shot but in the invisible, consistent habits that compound over time. By mastering these, "You don't just chase success—you become it."

CHAPTER TWO

PUBLIC PRODUCTIVITY MYTHS

Myths surrounding productivity negatively impact our mental and physical health. Recognizing and correcting these myths is the first step to creating a more effective system of work-life balance.

Myth 1: Productivity is Boosted Through Multitasking

One of the most common misconceptions is that multitasking makes you more productive. However, research states that multitasking diminishes overall productivity as it increases the chance of making mistakes and raising the stress levels. Instead of carrying out multiple activities at once, focusing on one activity at a time enhances the attention span which results in greater quality work.

Myth 2: Working Longer Hours is More Productive

This is another very popular myth that if one works longer hours, they will be more productive. Truthfully, if people are forced to work for long hours without breaks, they will ultimately lead to burn-out and decreased work quality. Strengthening focus and performance can be achieved by effectively prioritizing tasks and taking necessary breaks.

Myth 3: Being Actively Busy is Equal to Being Productive

The mix-up between activity and productivity is a common one. To be more productive, one needs to make use of their resources effectively. People should plan for rest and breaks to ensure that they are able to remain productive and creative over more extended periods of time. It has been proven that regular breaks lead to improved creative thinking, along with enhanced productivity.

Myth 4: Success habits can be imitated

Adopting the habits of very successful people can serve as motivation, but the truth is, these practices do not work for everyone. An individual is better off modifying habits for their own particular situation rather than exercise other people's habits as they are.

Myth 5: More work means more output

Working on a lot of activities does not mean one is as productive as one can be, this statement overlooks the value of the tasks being accomplished. Withdrawal deeper on core issues which are of high priority will yield much more value than just going through the motions of completing the tasks on the list.

Having discussed these previously held beliefs, let us now shift our focus to more logical approaches to productivity, enabling them to formulate plans that suit their abilities and situations for enhanced and meaningful achievement.

CHAPTER THREE

Neuroscience of Focus & Motivation

Appreciating the neuroscience of motivation and focus clarifies the complex mechanisms that support our capacity to sustain attention and engage with goal-directed behaviours. At the heart of this process sits a vital change in mindset and method- Neurotransmitters in the mind key for regulating motivation and attention, that take central parts in leading attention and motivation.

Dopamine's Role in Motivation- Dopamine, is the "feel-good" neurotransmitter, it is crucial for motivation. It released in the response to pleasing stimuli, reinforcing behaviour that leads to positive outcomes. This release also helps to increase our sense of pleasure, strengthening the neural pathways related with goal-directed behaviours, which makes us more likely to repeat actions that result in rewards.

Role of Norepinephrine in focus- Another vital neurotransmitter that is compulsory for concentration and focus is norepinephrine. It upgrades our capacity to focus on activities by hovering mindfulness and priming the brain to react to inputs. Higher norepinephrine levels are associated to better cognitive function, especially while doing tasks that demand for prolonged focus.

Portion of the Brain that is Concerned:

Prefrontal Cortex- Executive functions, including as planning, decision-making, and social behaviour regulation, are within this domain. It is crucial for nourishing concentration and directing motivation.

Basal Ganglia: Engaged in habit formation and restitution processing, the basal ganglia strengthen behaviours that lead to positive outcomes, thereby influencing motivation.

Anterior Cingulate Cortex: This region is linked with error detection and emotional regulation, contributing to nonstop attention and motivation.

First understand your mind-set and allow for strategies to boost concentration and determination

Engaging in mindfulness meditation can rise norepinephrine levels, thereby improving attention and focus. Then by setting clear goals, achievable goals can excite dopamine release, supporting motivation and inspiring persistence. And even by doing Regular physical activity has been shown to boost both dopamine and norepinephrine levels, enhancing mood and cognitive function."

Time vs. Energy Management

CHAPTER FOUR

WHY MANAGING ENERGY IS MORE IMPORTANT THAN TIME

You must hear about the technique of **"Battery analogy"**- Human energy levels are equal to those of a smartphone battery, which continues extensive when appropriately charged and power-saving techniques are used. You also heard about "Quality over Quantity" and "Energy-Boosting vs Energy-Draining Tasks", Right?

While time is a fixed resource, energy is dynamic and fluctuates throughout the day. "Managing energy is more important than managing time because energy determines how effectively we use the hours we have". The human body operates on a biological rhythm called the Ultradian cycle, which dictates periods of high focus followed by natural dips in energy. Research in neuroscience shows that the brain can focus intensely for 90 to 120 minutes before requiring a break to replenish mental resources. Ignoring these natural cycles and forcing productivity beyond optimal energy levels leads to decision fatigue, burnout, and lower efficiency.

Energy management can be seen mostly in professional athletes. "Elite marathon runners like Eliud Kipchoge do not simply train for longer hours but instead focus on maximizing recovery and optimizing energy output". They follow strict schedules where training is balanced with plenty of rest, nutrition, and mental recovery to ensure peak performance. Similarly, knowledge workers and entrepreneurs should align their most demanding cognitive tasks with their highest energy periods rather than simply working long hours.

Take the circumstance of a corporate executive who works 12-hour a day but constantly feels exhausted, struggling with declining productivity. By shifting focus from time management to energy management, they redesign their schedule based on their natural energy peaks—tackling deep-thinking work in the morning, scheduling routine tasks during afternoon nose-dives, and prioritizing movement and short breaks for sustained energy. Studies show that employees who take regular breaks experience a 45% increase in work engagement compared to those who push through exhaustion.

Another scientific principle that supports energy management is the mitochondrial function—our body's ability to produce ATP (the energy currency of cells). Poor lifestyle choices such as lack of sleep, poor diet, and inactive habits drain cellular energy, reducing productivity despite having enough time. High achievers like Jeff Bezos prioritize sleep and exercise, knowing that peak cognitive performance depends on high energy levels rather than simply extending working hours.

Ultimately, managing energy instead of obsessing over time allows individuals to work smarter, not harder. By understanding natural productivity rhythms, fuelling the body with proper nutrition, and optimizing rest and movement, people can accomplish more in less time without burning out.

CHAPTER FIVE

The Role of Sleep, Nutrition, and Exercise

Most people focus on time management but completely ignore energy management. And what fuels your energy? Sleep, nutrition, and exercise. If you're constantly tired, eating junk, and barely moving, no productivity hack in the world will save you. High achievers understand that their brain and body are their greatest assets, and if they don't take care of them, their work suffers. Think about it: Have you ever tried to power through an important task on just four hours of sleep? It feels like dragging yourself through quicksand. Science backs this up—sleep deprivation leads to a 40% drop in cognitive performance, weakens memory, and kills creativity. Your brain needs deep sleep to repair itself, process information, and get you ready for the next day. Jeff Bezos, one of the most successful entrepreneurs, swears by getting at least eight hours of sleep every night, and he credits it for his clear decision-making.

Now, let's talk about what you put into your body. Food isn't just about filling your stomach; it's fuel for your brain. Ever noticed how sluggish you feel after a fast-food binge? That's because processed foods spike your blood sugar, giving you a quick high, followed by a crash. If you're living on caffeine and sugar just to survive the day, your energy levels will always be unstable. On the other hand, nutrient-rich foods like protein, healthy fats, and complex carbs give you steady energy and mental clarity. Omega-3s, found in foods like salmon and walnuts, are known to boost brain function and reduce mental fatigue. Steve Jobs was famous for his disciplined eating habits, often consuming a fruit-based diet to keep his mind sharp. It's no coincidence that what you eat directly affects how you think, feel, and perform.

And then there's exercise—the most underrated productivity hack. You don't need to become a gym freak, but if you're not moving your body, you're draining your energy. Exercise increases blood flow to the brain, releases endorphins (your natural mood boosters), and reduces stress. Even a short 20-minute walk can wake you up more effectively than another cup of coffee. Studies show that people who exercise regularly are 15% more productive than those who don't. Richard Branson, the founder of Virgin Group, credits his daily workouts for giving him an extra four hours of high-energy work every day.

Here's the reality: You can't work smart if you're exhausted, sluggish, or mentally drained. So prioritize sleep, eat like your brain depends on it (because it does), and move your body daily. Do this consistently, and you'll notice a massive shift in your energy, focus, and overall performance.

CHAPTER SIX

FINDING YOUR PEAK PRODUCTIVITY HOURS

Have you ever noticed that some parts of the day feel effortless, while others feel like you're dragging yourself through mud? That's because not all hours are created equal. Your brain doesn't operate at 100% capacity from morning till night—it has natural peaks and dips in energy. If you want to work smarter, not harder, you need to figure out your peak productivity hours—the time when your focus, creativity, and efficiency are at their highest. Most people try to force productivity at the wrong times, which leads to frustration, burnout, and wasted effort. But what if you could align your toughest tasks with your natural high-energy periods? That's how top performers get more done in less time.

Now, here's the science behind it. Your body follows a natural rhythm called the circadian cycle, which controls your energy levels throughout the day. Some people are morning larks—they wake up early, feel sharp in the morning, and lose steam by afternoon. Others are night owls, coming alive in the evening when most people are winding down. And then there's a third group, the in-betweeners, who peak in the late morning or early afternoon. The key is to stop fighting your natural rhythm and use it to your advantage. Instead of scheduling deep work when your brain is half-asleep, tackle it during your peak hours. A famous example? Elon Musk. He structures his day in short, focused sprints, scheduling deep-thinking tasks during his peak mental hours and leaving emails or meetings for his lower-energy periods.

So, how do you find your own peak productivity hours? It's simple: track your energy levels for a week. Keep a journal or use a time-tracking app to note when you feel the most focused, creative, and alert. Look for patterns—do you get a rush of energy at 10 AM? Do you crash around 3 PM? Once you've identified your natural highs and lows, you can structure your work around them. For example, if you're a morning person, tackle your most demanding work—strategy planning, writing, problem-solving—before lunch. Leave meetings, admin work, or routine tasks for when your energy dips. If you're a night owl, flip the schedule—do creative work in the evening and save the morning for easier tasks.

Another trick? Protect your peak hours like gold. That means no distractions, no unnecessary meetings, and no mindless scrolling on your phone. Block off this time in your calendar, set boundaries, and let people know you're unavailable. High achievers guard their peak hours fiercely because they know that one hour of deep, focused work is worth three hours of distracted work. And if you're worried about having a strict 9-to-5 job, don't stress—just make small tweaks where possible. Maybe you can shift your toughest tasks to align with your peak energy levels, or use breaks strategically to recharge before tackling another deep work session.

At the end of the day, productivity isn't about working all the time—it's about working at the right time. Once you discover your peak productivity hours and use them wisely, you'll get more done in less time, with less stress, and more energy left for what truly matters.

The Psychology of
Procrastination

WHY WE DELAY TASKS

Candidly speaking—procrastination isn't just about being lazy. We've all done it, putting things off, making excuses, and suddenly deciding that reorganizing the entire closet is more important than tackling that one task we've been avoiding. But why? Why do we delay things we know we need to do? It's not just about time management; it's something deeper—it's psychological. At its core, procrastination is usually about fear. Fear of failure, fear of not doing it perfectly, fear of judgment. How many times have you hesitated to start something just because you were worried it wouldn't turn out right? Our brains fool us into thinking that delaying a task will somehow make it easier, but in reality, we're just avoiding the discomfort of starting. And the longer we avoid it, the bigger and scarier it feels, like a snowball rolling downhill until suddenly we're buried under stress and regret. But here's something you might not have considered—procrastination is also about dopamine. Our brains crave pleasure and avoid discomfort, so when faced with something challenging, we instinctively look for something easier and more enjoyable. That's why scrolling through social media, binge-watching a show, or snacking feels so appealing in the moment. These things give us an instant dopamine hit, tricking us into feeling like we're accomplishing something when really, we're just putting off what actually matters.

And then there's perfectionism—the sly villain of productivity. Many of us procrastinate because we have ridiculously high standards. If something doesn't feel like it'll be perfect, it's easier to avoid it altogether. But ironically, procrastination often leads to rushed, last-minute work, which is the exact opposite of perfect. It's a vicious cycle—we tell ourselves we're just "waiting for the right time," but let's be real, that perfect moment never actually comes. And don't forget decision fatigue. Ever felt so overwhelmed by everything on your to-do list that you end up doing... nothing? That's your brain running out of decision-making energy. The more choices we face, the harder it is to start anything. So instead of picking one task and diving in, we freeze, mindlessly scrolling, feeling guilty but still unable to take action.

So, how do we break free from this cycle? First, recognize that procrastination isn't a character flaw—it's just a habit, and habits can be changed. Start by setting small, achievable goals. Instead of telling yourself, "I need to finish this entire project," say, "I'll just write one sentence." Once you start, momentum kicks in. Next, eliminate distractions—put your phone in another room, close unnecessary tabs, turn off the TV. If you create a focused environment, you'll be less tempted to procrastinate. And most importantly, forgive yourself. Beating yourself up over past procrastination only makes it worse. Instead, acknowledge it, reset, and move forward. Procrastination is really a tug-of-war between your present self and your future self. Right now, you want comfort. But future you want results. The trick is making choices that benefit your future self, even if they feel uncomfortable in the moment. Because once you push past that initial resistance, action gets easier. And before you know it, the task that once seemed impossible is done—and you're wondering why you didn't start sooner.

CHAPTER EIGHT

UNDERSTANDING WILLPOWER AND DISCIPLINE

Let's have a real talk about willpower and discipline—two concepts we hear about all the time but rarely stop to truly understand. A lot of people think willpower means muscling through temptations, like saying no to cake or forcing yourself out of bed at 5 AM. Others think discipline is about strict routines and a life without flexibility. But here's the real deal—willpower and discipline aren't about making life miserable. They're about making things easier on yourself in the long run.

Think of willpower like a phone battery—it drains throughout the day. Every little decision you make, every distraction you resist, every time you push yourself to stay focused, you're using up that battery. That's why by the end of the day, you're more likely to grab fast food or zone out on your phone instead of doing something productive. This is where discipline steps in. Discipline isn't about fighting yourself all the time; it's about setting up smart systems so you don't have to rely on willpower as much. If you don't want to waste time on social media, delete the app. If you want to wake up early, fix your bedtime first. Small changes like these keep you from draining your willpower on unnecessary battles.

A big mistake people make is thinking they need willpower to start. Nope. Action comes first, motivation follows. The hardest part of any task is just getting started, but once you do, you build momentum. Think of it like pushing a heavy boulder—getting it moving is tough, but once it starts rolling, it gets easier. So don't sit around waiting to "feel ready." Just take that first small step, no matter how imperfect it is.

And here's the thing—self-discipline doesn't mean beating yourself up when you mess up. You're human. Some days will be off. Some days you'll slip up, and that's okay. The goal isn't perfection; the goal is consistency. If you miss a workout or eat something unhealthy, don't fall into the trap of "Well, I messed up, so I might as well give up." No. Just reset and keep going. Progress isn't about being flawless—it's about bouncing back quickly and sticking with it.

So, what's the takeaway? Willpower is a limited resource, but discipline is your long-term strategy. Build habits that reduce unnecessary decision-making, take action before you feel ready, and most importantly, be kind to yourself along the way. Over time, what once felt impossible will start to feel natural, and that's when you know you've truly mastered discipline. Real change doesn't happen overnight, but with consistency, it happens before you know it.

CHAPTER NINE

PRACTICAL STRATEGIES TO OVERCOME PROCRASTINATION

Procrastination—it's something we've all battled at some point. We delay tasks, push deadlines, and tell ourselves we'll do it later, even when we know we shouldn't. And let's be practical—most of the time, it's not because we're lazy or incapable. It's deeper than that. As it often rooted in fear of failure, fear of not meeting expectations, or even fear of stepping out of our comfort zones. Sometimes, it's just the sheer weight of the task that overwhelms us, making us feel like we don't even know where to start. But the thing is —procrastination is a habit, not a personality trait, and like any habit, it can be broken.

One of the biggest reasons we procrastinate is that we see tasks as big, intimidating monsters. Our brains get stuck on how huge and time-consuming something feels, so we put it off. The key? Shrink the task. Instead of thinking,

"I have to write an entire report," just start with the first sentence. Instead of "I need to clean the whole house," focus on one corner of a room. Once you take that small step, it's easier to keep going. Momentum is powerful, and getting started is often the hardest part.

Another way to outsmart procrastination is to create a sense of urgency. Deadlines given by someone else push us to act, but what about tasks without external pressure? That's where self-imposed deadlines come in. Tell yourself, "I have 30 minutes to get as much done as possible," and watch how much more productive you become. Setting a timer, makes the task feel like a challenge rather than a chore. Then there's the environment factor. If your surroundings are full of distractions, of course, you're going to procrastinate. Your phone, social media, and even background noise can pull you away from what you need to do. Make things easier on yourself by designing a workspace that encourages focus. Put your phone in another room, close unnecessary tabs, and set up a designated work area that tells your brain, "This is where I get things done."

Now, let's talk about the mental side of procrastination. One of the biggest lies we tell ourselves is, "I'll feel more like doing this later." Spoiler alert: you won't. Waiting for motivation is like waiting for the perfect weather to start running—you'll be waiting forever. Instead of relying on motivation, build discipline. Make showing up a habit, even if it's just for five minutes. Action creates motivation, not the other way around. And here's something we don't often realize—procrastination isn't just about avoiding work; it's about avoiding discomfort. We put off tasks because they feel hard, boring, or stressful. The Move? Change the way you look at them. Find ways to make tasks more enjoyable.

Play music while working, turn it into a game, or reward yourself afterward. If something feels less like a punishment, you'll be more likely to do it.

At the end of the day, overcoming procrastination isn't about forcing yourself to be more productive—it's about understanding why you procrastinate in the first place and making small, intentional changes. It's about making tasks feel easier, creating structure, and showing up even when you don't feel like it. And the best part? The more you practice beating procrastination, the less power it has over you. Before you know it, taking action will become second nature, and those things you used to put off will start getting done without hesitation.

Building a High-Performance Lifestyle

The Power of Morning Routines

The first 60 minutes of your day are crucial. It sets the tone for everything that follows, and trust me, how you start your day has a massive impact on how the rest of it unfolds. So, let's break it down and get into the details of what this time should look like.

First and foremost, waking up early is non-negotiable. I know it's tempting to hit that snooze button, but when you wake up late, something funny happens. You start feeling rushed, stressed, and that little voice in your head starts telling you it's too late to do the things you actually want to do, like exercising, reading, or even meditating. Suddenly, your day is already off track, and you're just trying to catch up. If you wake up early, you're in control. You've got time to do whatever feels right for you, whether it's hitting the gym, reading a book, or simply sitting in silence to collect your thoughts. This time gives you the freedom to start your day with intention and boosts your energy levels in a way that carries you through the rest of your day.

Now, let's talk about what you put into your body as soon as you wake up. A big one here is drinking green tea instead of coffee or regular tea. I know, I know, some of you are probably groaning right now. Coffee lovers, I see you! But here's the thing: drinking coffee early in the morning, especially between 6-10 AM, can actually mess with your body's natural rhythm. Your body naturally produces high levels of cortisol, the stress hormone, during this time, helping you feel awake and alert. If you drink coffee on top of that, it sends your cortisol levels soaring, which leads to heightened stress and anxiety. The worst part? Your body starts to depend on that external caffeine boost, reducing your natural energy production. Over time, this means you'll need more and more caffeine just to feel awake, which isn't great for your long-term energy levels. Green tea, on the other hand, has a gentler effect and doesn't cause that cortisol spike, so it'll help you feel alert without putting your body under stress.

After hydrating with something gentle like green tea, the next step is getting your body moving. Exercise in the morning is a game-changer. And I'm not talking about spending hours at the gym (unless you want to, of course). It's all about getting your blood flowing and waking up your muscles. Even just 10-20 minutes of movement can make a huge difference. Whether it's stretching, yoga, or a quick jog around the block, getting your heart rate up releases endorphins—those feel-good chemicals that boost your mood and set you up for a positive day. The more consistent you are with your morning exercise routine, the easier it will be to wake up, and you'll start feeling more energized throughout the day.

It's also important to remember that morning exercise doesn't have to be intense to be effective. If you're someone who's not used to working out, starting slow is perfectly fine. You can do a few rounds of stretches, some light yoga, or even a walk around your neighborhood. The key here is consistency. Making this a daily habit will train your body to wake up with more energy and purpose.

In these first 60 minutes, it's all about setting your intentions. Wake up early, choose what feels right for you—whether it's meditation, exercise, or reading—and make sure you fuel your body with something that nurtures your energy. Avoid that morning coffee rush, and opt for green tea, which is gentler on your system. And remember, exercise doesn't have to be a huge time commitment. Start small, stay consistent, and watch how it transforms your energy, mood, and focus throughout the rest of the day. Your first hour sets the tone—make it count!

CHAPTER ELEVEN

MINDFULNESS, MEDITATION, AND GOAL SETTING

We've all been there—feeling stressed, heartbroken, or just overwhelmed by life. And I know, many of us turn to sleep, thinking it will be the quick fix to our troubles. For a while, it works, right? It gives us a break, a temporary escape from the chaos. But does it solving the problem? No right? Sleep doesn't solve the underlying issues. It doesn't address the stress, the heartbreak, or the emotional toll that's building up. So, what's the solution for a long-term effect? Meditation. Yes, meditation. I know, some of you might be thinking, "What's the point of sitting still when there's so much to do?" or "How can I meditate when my mind is racing?" It's a common thought, but meditation isn't just about relaxation. It's a powerful tool that helps to increase awareness, bring peace to your mind, and support your inner transformation.

You see, when we're stressed or unhappy, our bodies produce certain hormones that can drag us down. Take dopamine, for example. When our dopamine levels are low, we feel sad or stressed, and our motivation takes a hit. Dopamine is what encourages us to take action toward our goals and gives us that sense of pleasure when we achieve them. So, how do we boost dopamine? Meditation can help. By calming the mind, it creates space for our brain to reset and produce those feel-good chemicals, helping us move closer to our goals.

But what should we focus on during meditation? The answer is simple: the present moment. You don't need to empty your mind. That's not the goal. Meditation isn't about silencing your thoughts; it's about observing them, without judgment, and letting them pass. Think of it as training your mind to focus on what matters right now. And while meditation doesn't provide instant gratification like scrolling through your phone or diving into a binge-watch session, its benefits are far-reaching. Over time, you'll experience better focus, emotional resilience, and a calmness that can help you navigate even the toughest days.

So, how does meditation calm the mind? When you meditate, you activate the parasympathetic nervous system—the part of your brain responsible for rest and relaxation. It's like giving your body a permission slip to chill out. The more you practice, the more your body becomes conditioned to enter that relaxed state, reducing stress and anxiety while clearing mental fog.

In today's world, it's easy to get caught up in negative thinking. We're bombarded with stories of heartbreak, job disappointments, stress from our bosses, and social media overload. These constant waves of information don't leave us with time to reflect or process what's actually going on in our minds. Instead, they build frustration and stress. And let's be real: carrying that negativity isn't just draining emotionally; it takes a physical toll as well. Negative energy clouds our judgment, exhausts us, and even weakens our health. Have you ever had a stressful day and felt completely drained afterward? That's your body reacting to all the negativity you're carrying.

Now, let's talk about setting goals in this chaotic world. With so much going on, it's easy to feel lost or like you're moving in circles. But setting clear, intentional goals is the antidote. It's like giving your mind a roadmap. Goal setting isn't just about writing down what you want to achieve; it's about aligning your energy and focus toward those goals. The science behind it is simple: when you set a goal, your brain activates the reward system, releasing dopamine, the very hormone that fuels motivation. This helps you stay on track and feel rewarded for each step you take toward achieving your dreams.

Meditation, goal setting, and focusing on the present are all interconnected. They help reduce stress, raise your energy, and get you on the path to living a more intentional, positive life. When you clear your mind, you make space for clarity, and when you set your goals with intention, you direct that clarity toward something meaningful. So, the next time you feel overwhelmed by the weight of the world, remember that meditation is a tool you can use to regain control, reduce stress, and boost your energy, all while guiding you toward the life you've always wanted.

Here we will do some meditation activities. Practice this exercise and see the metamorphosis:

- Close your eyes, sit straight.

- And think about the present, what you are doing, where you are sitting or what's there in your surroundings.

- Take a deep breath. Breath in and breath out. Pause for a while.

- Now again think what you have achieved in your life. Little to little things you can think (for example just think yes I completed my Bachelors, or I am working in this reputed company etc, and see here is the magic- you are feeling good).

Now if you are frustrated or stuck somewhere just imagine about the person or things you are irritated right now

- Think about the negative things about that person, which you already were thinking

- Now that negativity let go.

- Tell yourself am forgiving that person. Am releasing you from my thoughts You are not making me a stressful person anymore because I am forgiving you. Thank you whatever you have taught me in my life. Am grateful for that.

"Start forgiving and show gratitude actually impact to our life magically."

CHAPTER TWELVE

DEVELOPING A ROUTINE THAT WORKS FOR YOU

Developing a routine that truly works for you isn't about following a strict set of rules or trying to live someone else's schedule. It's about finding what makes you feel energized, productive, and at peace. So often, we get caught up in the idea that a "perfect" routine looks the same for everyone. But the thing is, routines should be personalized. They should reflect your unique goals, lifestyle, and energy patterns. When do you feel most active? Its different for everyone either its morning or night or in between. Start placing your most important tasks during those windows. It's about working with your natural rhythms, not against them.

Next, think about the habits you want to build. for me it's exercising more, reading every day, or setting aside time for deep work. Whatever it should be, be realistic. Start small, and gradually build on your successes. If you try to overhaul your entire routine at once, it's easy to get overwhelmed. Focus on one habit at a time, and once it feels natural, add another. As consistency is key, but so is flexibility. Life happens, and sometimes things won't go according to plan—and that's okay. Allow yourself the space to adjust without feeling guilty. The goal is progress, not perfection.

And don't forget to include rest, it's just as crucial as the work. A well-balanced routine has a mix of action and relaxation. It's not about working non-stop. When you take breaks and get enough sleep, your brain is better able to focus, think creatively, and tackle challenges with more energy. Have you ever heard about quick nap? This is the best enhancers of your energy. Yes in between you can skip from your routine to boost up your energy whatever you like you can do it but not more than 10-20min, otherwise again it will drain your productivity. Best Time to Nap? Between 1 PM - 3 PM (post-lunch dip) for maximum benefits without affecting nighttime sleep.

Ultimately, the best routine is one that feels authentic to YOU. It doesn't have to be packed with dozens of tasks or follow the latest trend. The power of a good routine lies in its simplicity and in how it supports your goals and well-being. Start where you are, build gradually, and most importantly, give yourself the grace to adjust as you go.

Eliminating Distractions & Enhancing Focus

CHAPTER THIRTEEN

UNDERSTANDING DEEP WORK & ITS BENEFITS

Deep work is a concept that has gained immense attention in recent years, and for a good reason. It's the ability to focus without distraction on a cognitively demanding task for an extended period. When you tap into this kind of focus, it's like you enter a flow state, where you're so engrossed in your work that time seems to disappear. This is the heart of deep work—being so present that you're not just completing tasks but creating something exceptional. And believe me, the benefits are huge. Not only does deep work lead to greater productivity, but it also opens the door to creating higher-quality output. It's like hitting that sweet spot in life where you get the best results with the least amount of time, because you're working with total focus.

Let's talk about the science behind it, because it's pretty mind-blowing. When you engage in deep work, your brain goes into high gear, activating areas that help you solve complex problems and think critically. This heightened state of concentration actually rewires your brain, improving your cognitive abilities over time. Your brain's neuroplasticity, or its ability to form new connections, strengthens, which means the more you practice deep work, the easier it becomes to enter that state of deep focus. Think about it—what you're doing is not just working hard, it's training your brain to be more efficient and smarter. Another exciting thing about deep work is its impact on your sense of achievement. Have you ever completed a task, looked back, and felt deeply proud of what you've done? That's because deep work creates a sense of satisfaction that shallow tasks just don't provide. The depth of engagement you experience leads to a sense of meaning in what you do. Instead of being distracted and jumping between tasks, you're fully immersed, and that immersion brings its own kind of reward.

But, in reality—it's not easy to stay in deep work mode. We live in an era of constant interruptions, with emails, social media, and phone notifications always fighting for our attention. The key to deep work is creating a focused environment, where distractions are minimized. It's about saying "no" to shallow work, like checking your inbox or mindlessly scrolling through social media, and making space for tasks that demand your full attention. You need to carve out time in your day where you're intentional about being present in your work. This isn't just about getting things done faster—it's about doing them in a way that truly enhances the quality of your life and your results. The Fact—deep work isn't just for work-related tasks. It can apply to anything that requires your undivided attention. Whether you're working on a creative project, learning a new skill, or simply reflecting, when you give something your full focus, you elevate your experience. It can feel incredibly fulfilling to know that you've spent your time doing something meaningful, without distractions pulling you away. So, if you want to achieve more and truly improve your performance, deep work is your secret weapon. It's about being intentional with how you spend your time, and in doing so, getting the best out of yourself. It's not about how many hours you work; it's about how deeply you engage with your tasks, and when you embrace this kind of focus, the results speak for themselves

CHAPTER FOURTEEN

Managing Digital & Environmental Distractions

We've all been there, right? You sit down to work, and within minutes, you find yourself checking your phone, scrolling through social media, or getting distracted. It feels almost impossible to focus when digital distractions are constantly pulling at your attention. And then there's the environment—loud noises, clutter, or even just the general chaos around you. These distractions are everywhere, and they're making it harder for us to do our best work. But why is it so difficult to focus, and what's happening in our brains when we get pulled away from a task?

The science behind these distractions is pretty fascinating. Our brains are wired to respond to new stimuli, which is why we're drawn to notifications and messages. Every time our phone buzzes or new notifications pop up, our brain gets a hit of dopamine—the "feel-good" chemical.

This reward system is powerful, and it keeps us coming back for more, even if we're in the middle of something important. The problem is that these distractions don't just take up our time; they also interfere with our cognitive abilities. Studies show that switching between tasks can reduce productivity and cognitive performance, a phenomenon known as "cognitive switching." When we jump from one task to another, we're not giving our brain enough time to fully engage with what we're doing, which leads to mistakes, slower progress, and mental fatigue.

But the digital world isn't the only culprit—our physical environment plays a massive role too. If you're trying to focus in a noisy room or surrounded by clutter, your brain is constantly processing all these irrelevant distractions. The more sensory input you have, the harder it becomes to focus on one thing. It's like trying to read a book while someone is playing loud music in the background. Your brain is fighting to tune out the noise, which only adds to the mental load. Research shows that cluttered spaces can increase stress and reduce your ability to concentrate. The visual clutter in your environment pulls your attention in many different directions, leaving you feeling scattered and overwhelmed.

So, how do we manage all these distractions? First, we need to understand that our brains are constantly seeking stimulation, but we have the power to control what we focus on. One effective strategy is to set boundaries for yourself—turn off notifications, silence your phone, or put it out of reach while you work. Give yourself permission to be fully present in the task at hand. You can also create a distraction-free environment by minimizing noise and keeping your workspace tidy. Simple things like closing the door or using noise-cancelling headphones can make a huge difference in your ability to concentrate. But here's the kicker—managing distractions isn't just about cutting things out. It's about replacing those distractions with something more meaningful. When you start focusing deeply on a task, you'll notice a shift. Instead of feeling like you're fighting against distractions, you'll feel like you're working with your brain's natural rhythms. This deep focus not only boosts your productivity but also gives you a sense of accomplishment and satisfaction, which is something those digital distractions can never offer. By recognizing the science behind distractions and actively taking steps to manage them, you'll be able to create a work environment that supports your best self. It's not about fighting your brain's impulses; it's about harnessing them and redirecting them toward something meaningful. When you eliminate the unnecessary distractions, you make space for deep, focused work that's more productive, more fulfilling, and ultimately, more aligned with your goals.

CHAPTER FIFTEEN

How to Build Concentration Stamina

Building concentration stamina is like developing a skill you can't live without, and it's one that, with practice, becomes second nature. We're not born with an endless supply of focus—our brains naturally want to wander, and the more we're exposed to distractions, the harder it becomes to maintain attention. But here's the secret: your brain can improve with the right training. When you focus, your brain lights up in ways that help you solve problems and engage deeply with your work. However, if you push it too far without a break, it runs out of steam. The good news is, you can gradually strengthen your brain's capacity for concentration, just like you would a muscle in the gym. A great way to start is by setting small, achievable focus sessions. Aim for 20 to 30 minutes of intense focus, then give yourself a well-deserved pause. This method works because your brain needs moments to recharge. Over time, you can increase these intervals, making it feel more natural and less overwhelming. This gradual build-up helps to prevent mental fatigue and allows you to focus for longer periods without feeling drained.

One of the biggest misconceptions is that to get better at concentrating, you need to push through tiredness. In reality, rest is a key player. Without proper sleep or downtime, your concentration will suffer. That's why ensuring you get quality rest is just as important as the work itself. Your brain needs to recover, refresh, and reset, and only then can it function at its peak. Regular exercise also helps—it increases oxygen flow to the brain, helping it stay sharp and improving cognitive function. Creating an environment that supports concentration is also crucial. If you're constantly shifting your attention between tasks, your brain has to work harder to stay focused. A cluttered, noisy space makes it even more difficult. It's all about reducing those distractions, setting boundaries, and creating a space where you can zero in on what you're doing. Building concentration stamina isn't just about forcing yourself to work longer. It's about consistency, knowing when to take breaks, and setting up a routine that respects your mind's capacity. With time, your brain will learn to sustain focus longer and more effectively, allowing you to dive deeper into tasks and perform at your best. Just remember, like any skill, concentration gets stronger with practice, rest, and the right environment.

The Role of Diet, Exercise & Sleep in Productivity

CHAPTER SIXTEEN

BRAIN-BOOSTING FOODS & HYDRATION

If you want your brain to function at its best, you need to feed it the right foods. Think of your brain like a high-performance engine—would you put cheap fuel in a sports car and expect it to run smoothly? Of course not! Yet, so many people survive on processed foods, excessive caffeine, and sugary snacks, then wonder why they feel sluggish, forgetful, or mentally drained. The fact is, what you eat and drink directly affects your focus, memory, mood, and overall brain function. If you want sharper thinking, better problem-solving skills, and sustained energy, it's time to pay attention to what's on your plate and in your glass. I used to overlook the power of food and hydration when it came to my own well-being, especially during stressful periods in my life. A while ago, I was constantly working long hours, barely eating, and surviving on caffeine and takeout. I felt mentally foggy, drained, and wasn't able to focus on anything for long. I started to skip breakfast for a while, thinking it wouldn't make much difference. But eventually, I noticed that it was affecting my productivity. I felt more lethargic, and even the smallest things started to annoy me. That's when I realized how important it is to start my day with a proper breakfast to keep my energy levels stable and my mood balanced.

That's when I decided to make a change. I began paying more attention to what I was putting into my body, especially since I knew I needed my mind to be at its sharpest to overcome everything going on in my life. I started with small changes—replacing sugary snacks with fruits like bananas and oranges, Eggs – A powerhouse of choline, which is crucial for memory and brain development. The yolk is where the magic happens, so don't skip it! These not only gave me a quick energy boost but also kept my brain fuelled with essential nutrients. Then Nuts (Almonds, Walnuts, Cashews) – Nuts, especially walnuts, are rich in vitamin E, which protects brain cells from oxidative stress. Walnuts also contain omega-3s, making them a double win for brain health. Pumpkin seeds – Loaded with magnesium, iron, zinc, and copper, which are essential for nerve function, learning, and protecting the brain from stress. I noticed that after eating them, I felt more focused and less sluggish. I also made sure to include more omega-3-rich foods like salmon and walnuts in my diet. Dark Chocolate (at least 70% cacao) – Yes, chocolate can be good for you! Dark chocolate contains flavonoids, caffeine, and antioxidants that enhance focus, improve mood, and increase blood flow to the brain. These healthy fats helped me feel more alert, and I could finally see some improvement in my concentration. Another game-changer for me was hydration. I wasn't drinking nearly enough water, so I began keeping a water bottle nearby at all times. Adding water-rich foods like cucumbers and watermelon into my meals helped me stay hydrated, and I instantly noticed my mental clarity improving. Instead of feeling tired and irritable, I began to feel more balanced and energized. Dehydration can reduce cognitive performance by 10-15%! That's why high achievers, from athletes to CEOs, prioritize hydration. So how much water do you really need? The standard rule is at least 8 glasses (2 liters) per day, but if you're active or live in a hot climate, you may need more. Coconut water, herbal teas, and water-rich fruits contribute to hydration. The key is to sip water throughout the day rather than chugging large amounts at once. One thing I've learned from all of this is how much my diet impacts my mental state. Eating well, prioritizing hydration, and fuelling my brain with the right foods have not only made me more productive, but it's also helped me feel more grounded and able to handle challenges—whether it's work or personal life. By taking care of my body and my brain, I was able to heal and come out of that tough period stronger. So, if you're feeling mentally drained or stuck, I really encourage you to take a look at what you're putting into your body. It's amazing how something as simple as eating the right foods and staying hydrated can make such a huge difference. Your mind is your greatest asset—give it the nourishment it deserves, and you'll notice sharper thinking, better memory, and higher energy levels.

"A well-fed, well-hydrated brain is an unstoppable brain!"

CHAPTER SEVENTEEN

EXERCISE ROUTINES FOR MAXIMUM ENERGY

If you've ever felt sluggish and drained, the last thing you probably wanted to do was exercise. Movement creates energy. It might sound strange, but science proves that the more you move, the more energy you generate. Exercise isn't just about losing weight or building muscle; it's one of the most powerful ways to increase stamina, sharpen focus, and boost overall productivity. Think about it—have you ever noticed how energized you feel after a good workout? That's because physical activity increases blood flow, oxygenates your brain, and triggers the release of endorphins—your body's natural energy boosters. The best part? You don't need to spend hours in the gym to reap the benefits. Just a few smart exercise routines can make a massive difference in how you feel throughout the day.

So, what types of exercises give you the biggest energy boost? Let's break it down.

Cardio Workouts (Running, Cycling, Jump Rope, Dancing) – When you engage in cardio, your heart rate increases, pumping more oxygen to your brain and muscles. This leads to higher endurance levels, better mental clarity, and improved mood.

Strength Training (Bodyweight Exercises, Weightlifting, Resistance Bands) – Lifting weights isn't just about building muscle; it trains your body to use energy more efficiently. Strength training increases your metabolism, meaning you burn more calories even when resting. It also enhances posture and reduces fatigue, making everyday tasks feel easier.

High-Intensity Interval Training (HIIT) – If you're short on time but need an energy surge, HIIT is your best friend. This workout involves short bursts of intense activity followed by brief rest periods, keeping your heart rate elevated and maximizing calorie burn. HIIT workouts have been proven to increase mitochondria production—these are the tiny power plants in your cells that create energy. More mitochondria = more energy!

Yoga and Stretching – While cardio and strength training build stamina, yoga and stretching help reduce stress and mental fatigue. Yoga increases flexibility, improves circulation, and activates the parasympathetic nervous system, which promotes deep relaxation. A simple 10-minute stretching routine in the morning can wake up your muscles and refresh your mind.

Breathwork & Movement (Tai Chi, Pilates, Deep Breathing Exercises) – Breathwork is a secret weapon for instant energy. Deep breathing techniques, like diaphragmatic breathing, increase oxygen flow to the brain and reduce stress hormones like cortisol. This is why elite athletes and CEOs use controlled breathing exercises before high-pressure situations—they stay calm, focused, and full of energy.

Science has shown that exercise increases brain-derived neurotrophic factor (BDNF), a protein that supports brain function and memory. It also regulates hormones like dopamine and serotonin, which improve motivation and happiness. If you feel exhausted all the time, it's not because you need more coffee—it's because your body craves movement. Start small, stay consistent, and make exercise part of your routine. You'll soon notice that instead of draining you, the right workouts will leave you feeling stronger, sharper, and more energized every single day.

CHAPTER EIGHTEEN

Sleep Hygiene & Its Impact on Performance

Most of us don't give sleep the respect it deserves. We sacrifice it for late-night scrolling, movies, or cramming in extra work, thinking we'll just "catch up on sleep later." But you can't cheat sleep. The quality of your sleep directly affects your focus, energy levels, memory, and even emotional well-being. If you've ever woken up feeling groggy, unfocused, or just "off," it's likely because your sleep hygiene needs improvement. Good sleep isn't just about the number of hours—it's about the quality of those hours.

Science proves that sleep is the foundation of peak performance. When you sleep, your brain goes through different stages, including deep sleep and REM sleep, both of which are crucial for recovery and cognitive function. Deep sleep is when your body repairs tissues, strengthens the immune system, and restores physical energy. REM sleep (the dream phase) is when your brain processes emotions, consolidates memories, and enhances creativity. If you don't get enough of these sleep stages, you'll struggle with concentration, decision-making, and even emotional control. So, how do you improve your sleep hygiene? It starts with building a nighttime routine that signals to your body that it's time to wind down. Here are some science-backed habits to optimize your sleep:

Stick to a Schedule – Your body thrives on routine. Going to bed and waking up at the same time—even on weekends—helps regulate your circadian rhythm, which controls your sleep-wake cycle.

Limit Blue Light Exposure – Your phone, laptop, and TV emit blue light, which tricks your brain into thinking it's still daytime. This suppresses melatonin, the hormone responsible for making you sleepy. Try using blue light filters or avoiding screens at least an hour before bed.

Create a Sleep-Inducing Environment – Your bedroom should be cool, dark, and quiet. Studies show that a room temperature between 60-67°F (16-19°C) promotes better sleep. Invest in blackout curtains, white noise machines, or even an eye mask if needed.

Avoid Stimulants Before Bed – Caffeine, nicotine, and even alcohol can disrupt sleep quality. Caffeine has a half-life of about 5-6 hours, meaning if you drink coffee in the late afternoon, it can still keep you wired at night. Instead, switch to herbal teas like chamomile or valerian root for relaxation.

Practice a Pre-Sleep Routine – Engage in calming activities like reading, journaling, meditating, or stretching. These helps reduce stress hormones like cortisol and signal to your brain that it's time to slow down.

"Treat sleep as a non-negotiable part of your success strategy, and you'll see the difference in every aspect of your life".

Mastering Time: Effective Planning Strategies

CHAPTER NINETEEN

The Pomodoro Technique, Eisenhower Matrix & Time Blocking

Effective time management relies on a structured approach to prioritize tasks, enhance focus, and maximize productivity. Three profound techniques-**The Pomodoro Technique, Eisenhower Matrix**, and **Time Blocking**-help individuals take control of their time while reducing stress and procrastination. It provides a systematic way to manage workload, stay away from distractions, and achieve long-term goals.

The Pomodoro Technique is a time management method articulated by Francesco Cirillo; whereby short intervals of focused work increase concentration. Set a timer for 25 minutes of intense work followed by 5 minutes of break time. After four cycles of Pomodoro, allow a longer, 15-30-minute break. This works particularly well for those who have a tendency toward procrastination and distraction. For example, if you are a freelance writer having a hard time meeting deadlines, you can stick to Pomodoro sessions so you can concentrate on writing without feeling overwhelmed. Knowing that taking a break is approaching, it helps keep the mind fresh and motivated, making tasks feel much more manageable. Time Blocking is another powerful strategy where time slots are formally allocated for different tasks in order to minimize contextual switching and optimize productivity. Unlike traditional to-do lists, time blocking instead obliges the individual to assign a specified time for, say, work, meetings, and breaks. For the software engineer, presented with numerous interruptions, he schedules his time from 9 to 11 AM for coding, from 11 to 12 noon to respond to emails, and from 1 to 3 PM for debugging and testing. As such, it sets a routine, thus minimizing distractions and creating an enhanced flow of work.

The Eisenhower Matrix helps to prioritize tasks by placing them into one of four quadrants: Urgent & Important (**do immediately**), Important but Not Urgent (**schedule**), Urgent but Not Important (**delegate**), and Neither Urgent nor Important (**eliminate**). For instance, a business owner juggling responsibilities may use the matrix to determine that dealing with customer problems (**urgent & important**) must be prioritized, while long-term strategy formulation (**important but not urgent**) requires scheduling. Alternatively, non-time-critical emails (**urgent but not important**) could be delegated to an assistant, while wasting time among social media (**neither urgent nor important**) could stand to be dropped from the task list altogether.

PRODUCTIVITY HACKS USED BY HIGH ACHIEVERS

Hear these words of wisdom: successful people enjoy stretchy productivity hacks that allow them to do more in less time while staying balanced. Rather than relying on sheer willpower, they utilize simple techniques to guide their focus and boost energy and efficiency. Those who do it well understand that productivity is all about working smarter, not harder-these techniques span from the 80/ 20 Rule to energy-based scheduling. Some 80/20 Rule (or Pareto Principle)-based 50-50 techniques rank as some of the best hacks other high achievers have used. Entrepreneurs and professionals can use this rule to stop wasting time on unproductive tasks and move on to those that add value. A good example would be Elon Musk, who uses this principle of concentrating on high-leverage activities, including product innovation and engineering, rather than wasting time with needless meetings. A general example would be any entrepreneur or professional who can analyze his daily tasks and put energy behind the few that offer the highest value.

Such an efficient operation is Energy-Based Scheduling, where tasks are arranged relative to the energy of individuals and not just time. High performers do not impose fixed schedules on themselves but front-end their toughest tasks to be performed when energy is at peak. Thus, for instance, Tim Cook of Apple gets up at 4:30 AM to do deep thinking before any kind of interference sets in. You may want to do your writing in the morning when you feel fresh and are your most efficient, and save the routine work for the afternoon when you tend to slow down. That is bound to provide optimal output without burnout.

The 2-Minute Rule is a productivity hack to keep the small tasks manageable in one's busy schedule. This rule is as simple as if a job takes less time than two minutes, do it without delay. Timely responses can be further exemplified by Jeff Bezos taking quick actions over short emails instead of accumulating them and therefore over more strategic decisions. This is a very easy rule to execute for small things like replying to emails, filing some papers or setting a quick telephonic meeting and saves huge time in future.

Time blocking and batching tasks also form part of the routine that high achievers follow. For instance, Oprah Winfrey batches her meetings and interviews on particular days of the week; she works in one project during the other days of the week. This helps to avoid constant context-switching which is very draining on mental energy. In the same vein, a content creator can assign Mondays for brainstorming, Tuesdays for filming, and Wednesdays for editing instead of doing all these tasks randomly throughout the week. Structure in itself brings efficiency and quality. Also, high achievers use Reverse Deadlines.

They set deadlines earlier than the actual due dates to avoid last-minute panic and to enhance quality. For instance, Warren Buffett usually makes investment decisions much earlier than the deadline because he wants to have time to think and change if necessary. A student using this technique might establish a personal deadline for an assignment two or three days before the real due date, ensuring plenty of time for revision.

Finally, a secret which few know about is that there is something referred to as a Not-to-Do List which enhances focus for high achieving people. It can be thought of as the inverse of a to-do list. It works by helping the creator understand the bad habits or unnecessary distractions that must not be done. For Mark Zuckerberg, wearing the same type of clothes as a means of simplifying his day-to-day choices works effortlessly. A professional might have their own list such as "No social media before lunchtime" or "Social media is banned throughout the day, except during lunch." This ensures that they stay productive throughout the entire workday. If one wish to achieve more productivity, they can try to implement these productivity hacks – removing bad habits, reverse deadlines, batch working, quick time management, avoiding multitasking, and rearranging schedules according to energy levels. These enable better workflow and higher output in less time. The key, however, lies in individualization and patience; the best people in the world also have specific strategies that work for them.

CHAPTER TWENTY-ONE

THE ART OF BATCHING & PRIORITIZATION

In order to make the best of our endeavours, we need to focus on the end result. This is where highly motivated people excel as they are fully aware of how to strengthen their concentration, cut inefficiencies, and conquer tasks. Task batching is one of the methods used by these goal-oriented individuals. It is the combination of grouping similar responsibilities and efficiently working on them within a certain time range while putting productivity first. These mechanisms, when applied together, help efficiently tackle workload and stress. The use of task batching is exceptionally effective when there is a need to minimize inefficient switching between tasks. The best part about this technique is that it allows the individual to remain in mental work mode throughout, aiming to achieve peak efficiency. For instance, a digital marketer who oversees social media handles may prefer to batch work on Instagram posts for a month in one day. As a result, there is a guarantee of efficient use of time as well as unified branding.

With further prioritization, the most critical activities are done first then everything else follows. The Eisenhower Matrix is a tool for prioritization which places equal importance on tasks that need to be completed into 4 quadrants: those which are urgent and important, those which are important but non-urgent, those which are urgent but not important, and those which are neither important nor urgent. A case in point is that a startup founder will schedule investor meetings that are important but not urgent after the completion of product development that is important and urgent, while at the same time outsourcing administrative work that is important but not urgent. Such focus aids in Morton's law and spending less time on low impact functions.

Another technique is the Ivy Lee Method which places utmost importance on tasks and is used by people who always get things done. It entails selecting six basic tasks every evening and completing them in order of priority on the succeeding morning. It was popularized by Charles Schwab, the American steel tycoon who revolutionized the steel industry, who also credited it for the success of his company. Students preparing for exams can also adapt this method by attending to the most difficult subjects first thereby allowing extra time for better focus.

Let's dive into one of the most productive combinations: batching and the Pomodoro Technique, which involves setting excessively focused intervals of 25 minutes. For instance, a creative can batch video recording for three hours by utilizing multiple Pomodoro as it provides an immense focus while making sure to take breaks between tasks. Within a short period, this will be highly beneficial for skinning burnout and increasing general productivity. By employing both tactics of batching and prioritization, one can make their workload easier, reducing decision fatigue while increasing productivity. All these strategies come in handy for ensuring maximum efficiency while one does not burn out be it a CEO of a billion-dollar company or a freelancer juggling multiple clients.

Setting SMART Goals & Tracking Progress

CHAPTER TWENTY-TWO

Turning Goals into Daily Actions and Importance of Measuring Progress

This technique I learnt from my roommate when I was staying in Hyderabad. She used to track her daily works - how much she did, what's new things she did, what she missed. Even though she used to track how much money she spent in a month. That time I didn't care about this technique much but later on I understand the value. Now you must be thinking what's this is about? So, we all make plans, but let's face it, how many times have you made plans just to forget about them a few weeks later? The problem isn't that we lack ambition; it's that we don't always set our goals in a way that sets us up for success. This is where SMART goals are useful. SMART stands for Specific, Measurable, Achievable, Relevant, and Time-bound. It's not just another productivity buzzword—it's a game-changer.

We all have goals—those big, exciting dreams that fill us with energy and motivation when we think about them. But in real—how often do those dreams turn into something perceptible? More often than not, we get stuck in the thinking phase and never move into action. And it's not because we don't care or because we're lazy—it's because we don't translate our goals into small, daily actions. You wouldn't expect to build a house in a day, right? You'd lay one brick at a time. That's exactly how achieving any goal works. The first key to making real progress is breaking your goal into bite-sized pieces. Building habits around your goals is a game-changer. If you say, "I want to stay in good physical shape" that's great—but it's also vague. How do you turn that into action? Instead of just hoping for results, commit to something clear: "I will go for a 20-minute run every morning before breakfast." Suddenly, your goal isn't some abstract wish—it's a daily action you can take. Small steps create momentum, and momentum keeps you moving forward.

Motivation is great, but it's unreliable. Some days you'll feel motivated, very energetic and other days you won't. That's why habits matter. When something becomes part of your routine, you don't need motivation—you just do it. Think about brushing your teeth. You don't debate whether or not to do it; you just do it because it's part of your day. That's how goals should be approached. If writing is your goal, don't wait for inspiration. Set a habit: "Every night at 8 PM, I will write for 30 minutes." The more automatic your actions become; the easier success gets. But let's talk about something people often overlook—tracking progress. One of the biggest reasons people give up on their goals is because they don't feel like they're making progress. But progress isn't always obvious. Sometimes, it's slow and subtle. That's why tracking is so powerful—it lets you see the changes happening over time, even when you don't feel them in the moment. Think about it: If you were on a road trip and had no map, you'd have no idea how far you'd come or how close you were to your destination. That's what happens when you don't track your progress—you feel lost, and it's easy to give up. But when you track even small wins, you start to see just how far you've come, and that keeps you motivated. Another crucial step? Be willing to adjust. Goals aren't set in stone. If something isn't working, change it. If your original plan to write 1,000 words a day is making you burn out, drop it to 500. If your workout routine isn't enjoyable, find a different exercise you love. Adjusting your approach doesn't mean you're quitting—it means you're being smart about what actually works for you. Another thing is that we need to wait for the "perfect time" to start. Spoiler—there is no perfect time. Life will always be busy, and obstacles will always exist. The best time to start? Right now. Small daily efforts may not feel like much in the moment, but over time, they add up in incredible ways. A single healthy meal won't transform your body, but consistently eating well will. Writing one page won't give you a book overnight, but writing daily will. The magic is in showing up consistently.

At the end of the day, turning goals into daily actions and tracking progress isn't just about getting things done—it's about creating a life you're proud of. It's about proving to yourself that you can set a goal, commit to it, and follow through. And trust me, once you see progress—even in the smallest form—you'll be hooked. Success isn't about luck or talent. It's about the daily choices you make. So, what's one small action you can take today to move toward your goal? Write it and tag me to my Instagram.

CHAPTER TWENTY-THREE

TOOLS & TECHNIQUES FOR PRODUCTIVITY TRACKING

So, how do you track progress effectively? There's no one right way—it depends on what works for you. Some people use **habit trackers**, marking off each day they complete their action. Others prefer **journaling**, writing a few lines about what they did and how they felt. Some use **productivity apps** to log their progress digitally. The method is the important part—what matters is that you're consistently checking in with yourself and recognizing your growth, which will give you more energy to work and day by day you will start to love your work. Because your daily progress will keep you cheering and excited!

First up—**habit tracking**. It's simple but incredibly effective. Whether it's a simple checklist, a bullet journal, or a habit-tracking app, marking off daily progress is surprisingly satisfying. It turns consistency into a visual reward. However, Habit tracking isn't just about ticking off boxes—it's like giving yourself a little high-five every day! The trick is to make it fun and personal. Instead of a boring checklist, try a **habit jar**—drop a bead or coin in every time you complete a habit and watch it fill up. Use **color-coded calendars** to visually track your progress; the more colors, the better! If you love surprises, write small rewards on sticky notes and pick one randomly after a streak. Keep a **"Why I Started" page** in your journal to remind yourself on tough days. Make it social—challenge a friend or even give your habits funny names (like "Water Warrior" for drinking more water). Take pictures of your progress and make a "before & after" collage. And most importantly, **celebrate small wins**—because every step counts, even the messy ones!

Time-Blocking – If you find yourself procrastinating, scheduling your tasks into specific time slots can help. When you assign time to a task, it feels more real and less like something you'll "get to later." The thing is Time blocking isn't about packing your day with tasks—it's about owning your time like a boss! Think of it as creating a personalized schedule where every task has its own VIP slot. Instead of a boring to-do list, theme your days (like "Creative Mondays" or "Chill Sundays") to keep things fresh. Use color-coded blocks in your planner or digital calendar so you can instantly see where your focus goes. Try the Power Hour Method, where you dedicate one solid hour to deep work with no distractions. Block time for breaks too—because rest is just as productive! If you're easily distracted, set a "No Interruptions" zone during your most important blocks. Use alarms or music playlists to signal when it's time to switch tasks. And remember, it's not about perfection—it's about progress, one well-planned block at a time!

The Weekly Review – Every week, take a few minutes to check in with yourself. What went well? What didn't? What adjustments can you make? This reflection helps you stay on track and transformation your approach if needed. A weekly review isn't just about looking back—it's about levelling up for the week ahead! Think of it as a quick reset button to keep life from feeling like a chaotic mess. Start by celebrating wins, no matter how small (yes, even drinking enough water counts!). Then, reflect on what worked and what didn't—were you productive or just "busy"? Rate your week from 1 to 10 and jot down what could've made it better. Scan your to-do list and move unfinished tasks forward (or ditch them if they don't matter anymore). Set 1-3 priorities for next week so you stay focused on what truly matters. If you journal, write down a few thoughts or lessons learned. End with a little self-care—whether it's a treat, a nap, or a dance party in your room. A weekly review should feel refreshing, not like homework!

Goal-Setting Apps -The key is to not just set goals, but to map out how you'll achieve them. Goal-setting apps aren't just about tracking progress—they're about turning your dreams into action! Think of them as your personal coach, right in your pocket. You can use some free version apps like **Todoist** or **Trello** to break down big goals into bite-sized tasks, making them feel less overwhelming. For those who love visual motivation, apps like **Habitica** turn goal-setting into a game—complete tasks and earn rewards. **Strides** lets you track multiple goals at once, helping you stay on top of everything from fitness to finances. If you're into reflection, **Way of Life** helps you log your habits and see your progress over time. And for anyone who likes a little accountability, **Stickk** lets you commit to goals with real consequences if you don't follow through! Choose the app that speaks to you and make it part of your routine—it'll keep you motivated and on track, one tap at a time.

The Power of Saying No: Setting Boundaries

THE HIDDEN COSTS OF OVER-COMMITMENT

Overcommitment. We've all been there, haven't we? It's like a never-ending stream of "Yes!" responses, each one feeling like a small victory at the time. But before long, we're trapped in the "Yes Trap," where saying yes to everything leaves us stretched too thin. Sure, it feels good to help everyone, to be the go-to person, the reliable one. But here's the thing: constant yes-ing doesn't make you a superhero. It makes you a stressed-out, overwhelmed version of yourself, barely holding it all together, sometimes you might think people taking advantage of you or taking your for granted, later you will feel so drained that it will affect you gravely. Let me paint a picture. You've said yes to a work project, agreed to babysit for a friend, committed to organizing a family event, and promised to join a fitness group—all in the same week. It sounds like you're juggling it all, right? But what's happening inside? Stress builds up like a snowball, and soon, resentment creeps in. You're resenting the very people you said yes to, and, more tragically, you start resenting yourself for not having set boundaries. This is where the "Energy Drain Effect" kicks in. Think about it. Mentally, emotionally, physically—you're depleted. You're running on fumes, and when the time comes to focus on something that really matters, you have nothing left to give. Imagine you've got a crucial meeting at work, but you're too tired to prepare. Or you're so emotionally drained from helping others that when it's time for self-care, you just can't find the energy to even think about it. It's a friend story of mine- I noticed something about my friends who always seemed to take on a little too much. Whenever we'd hang out, we'd invite him, but he'd often say he had work or other things to take care of. Because of this overcommitment he messed up so many things, he used to pile up every undo-work and later he felt stressed and burn out. Even when he was planning a trip with his friends, he ended up organizing the whole thing. It's great that he wanted to help, but when you're in a group, it's okay to share the responsibility. During the trip, I could tell he was feeling a bit worn out, and I noticed he wasn't as excited as he usually is. It seemed like he already knew every detail of what was coming next, and there wasn't that element of surprise or joy in the moment. I tried to mention this to him, but he didn't quite understand, he misunderstood me. It felt like he was so focused on making sure everything was perfect that he missed out on the simple, spontaneous moments that can make a trip truly memorable. It made me realize that sometimes, it's okay to let go a little and just enjoy the experience, rather than trying to control every part of it.

What if, instead of overloading your schedule, you focused on fewer things and did them really well? It's all about Quality Over Quantity. When you say yes to fewer things, you can pour your energy into those commitments, give them your full attention, and excel. Imagine the power of doing just one thing at a time with excellence. Isn't that more satisfying than running from task to task with mediocre results? Quality brings you pride, growth, and the ability to fully invest in your work, relationships, and self. Now, let's talk about something that sneaks up on us—the Invisible Opportunity Costs. Every time you say "yes" to something, you're unknowingly saying "no" to something else. It might be time to relax, an opportunity to work on your personal goals, or a chance to enjoy a quiet evening with yourself. These are the things we often overlook, but they matter. By constantly giving away your time and energy, you're unknowingly sacrificing the things that truly nourish your soul. A hard truth: overcommitment is a thief. It steals time from you, yes, but it also robs you of the opportunity to grow. It's a trap that makes us think we're doing the right thing by saying yes to everyone, but it's actually keeping us stuck in a cycle of stress, burnout, and mediocrity. When you say yes to everything, you're holding yourself back from saying yes to the things that will move you forward. So, let's start by acknowledging that our time is limited. Every moment we say yes to something, we're choosing what to prioritize. You don't have to be everything to everyone. It's okay to say no. It's okay to step back and let others step up. Your worth is not defined by your ability to constantly be available, to say yes to every request, or to keep adding things to your plate.

Next time you feel that pull to say yes, pause and ask yourself: What's the cost? Will saying yes bring you closer to your goals, or will it drain your energy, time, and joy? Saying no to some things doesn't mean you're failing; it means you're getting better at investing in the things that truly matter to you. Remember, life is not about filling every slot in your calendar; it's about making the most of the time you have. Instead of rushing to say yes, why not try saying, "Let me think about it"? Give yourself the space to reflect on what really aligns with your priorities. Start saying yes to yourself, to your growth, to the things that will nourish you and move you forward. Overcommitment is a sneaky little monster that loves to disguise itself as productivity or helpfulness. But let me tell you: the real productivity comes from saying no to the unimportant, so you can say yes to the things that truly matter. And trust me—once you get the hang of it, it feels amazing to be in control of your time, your energy, and your life. So, let's stop saying yes out of obligation and start saying yes to what truly serves us. Your energy is precious. Don't let it be drained by things that don't move you forward. Quality over quantity. And remember, the best opportunities come when you stop trying to do everything and start doing the right things well.

CHAPTER TWENTY-FIVE

How to Set Personal & Professional Boundaries

Setting boundaries can be one of the most freeing yet uncomfortable things you can do for yourself. If you're anything like me, you might've spent years trying to please everyone around you, never wanting to let anyone down. But here's the thing: boundaries are not selfish. They're essential. They're the invisible lines we draw in the sand to protect our energy, time, and mental well-being. Without them, we risk burning out, feeling overwhelmed, and losing ourselves in the process. So, let's talk about how we can set these boundaries in a way that feels real and natural.

The Power of Clear Communication: When it comes to boundaries, clear communication is your best friend. People can't read your mind (no matter how much we might wish they could!). If something's bothering you or you feel like your time or energy is being stretched too thin, the only way anyone will know is if you speak up. If you're overthinking something, whether it seems minor or major, don't keep it to yourself—just share it. Avoid making assuming things like, "What if they don't get it?" By communicating openly and explaining your concerns respectfully, people will be able to understand, and any misunderstandings can be cleared up, allowing you to relax and feel more at peace. If you pile up your thinking it not only will make you irritate but also make your energy drained. Now, I know it's easy to feel guilty or awkward about saying no or asking for space, but here's the secret: people who truly respect you won't mind. A simple, "Hey, I need some quiet time to recharge tonight," or, "I can't take on any more projects this week," goes a long way without being harsh. It's not about being strict; it's about being honest. Setting boundaries isn't just for your benefit—it teaches others how to treat you. And once you get into the habit of clearly stating your limits, it becomes a lot easier. I promise, no one will think you're rude for protecting your peace.

Recognizing Manipulation Tactics: Let's face real—sometimes, people will try to manipulate you into crossing your own boundaries. They might do this knowingly, or they might not even realize they're doing it. Ever had someone say, "Oh, but we're friends, I thought you'd help me out," or "I'm really counting on you for this—can you please do it this one time?" These are classic manipulation tactics, designed to make you feel guilty for saying no. Here's what I've learned: It's okay to say no. No one has the right to make you feel responsible for their emotions or their needs. You don't have to overexplain yourself or feel bad about it. Recognizing manipulation is the first step in taking back control of your time and your boundaries. Trust me, when you start saying no and standing firm, the people who truly care about you will respect that decision, and those who don't, well, sorry to say they're not your people.

Boundary Building Exercises: Now, let's talk about how you can start building these boundaries. It's not something that happens overnight—it's a practice. But like any new habit, the more you work on it, the easier it gets. So, begin small. Start with boundaries you can implement in your everyday life. For example, maybe it's deciding not to check phone after a certain time in the evening or taking a break during the day to walk outside and clear your head. Little things like that can make a huge difference in how you feel. You don't have to make dramatic changes right away. Once you get comfortable with the small boundaries, you can start setting bigger ones in your relationships or your job. It could be telling your boss that you're not available on weekends or telling a friend that you need some alone time after a busy week. Setting boundaries in your relationships can be tough, especially if you've been a people-pleaser for years, but it's about showing yourself the love and respect you deserve. It doesn't make you a bad person; it makes you someone who values their own time and energy.

One important thing to remember is that boundaries are not rigid or fixed. They can evolve. As your life changes, so do your boundaries, and that's completely okay. Maybe you need more time for yourself when life gets hectic or less time when you feel energetic. You get to decide what feels right for you, and you can adjust as needed. And don't feel guilty about it. Sometimes you have to put yourself first, and that's not a bad thing. In fact, it's the best thing you can do for your mental and emotional health. Another thing about boundaries is that they're not just about saying no to others—they're about saying yes to yourself. They're about giving yourself permission to rest, to breathe, to take care of what's important to you. It's okay to take breaks, to cancel plans, to put your phone down, and to prioritize your needs. When you do this, you're not just setting limits with others, but you're also teaching yourself how to live authentically and without guilt. At the end of the day, setting boundaries is about **"Self-respect"**. It's about valuing your time, your feelings, and your mental health. It's about knowing that you deserve to take up space and that it's okay to say no when something doesn't feel right. It's not easy, but with practice, it becomes second nature. So, go ahead—start small, speak up for yourself, and remember that you don't have to be everything to everyone. You just have to be enough for yourself.

CHAPTER TWENTY-SIX

AVOIDING BURNOUT WHILE STAYING PRODUCTIVE

Burnout is real, and it sneaks up on you when you least expect it. One minute, you're pushing through your to-do list, feeling like a productivity machine, and the next, you're drained, irritable, and questioning why you even started. I've been there—more times than I'd like to admit. I remember this one week where I had way too much on my plate—work deadlines piling up, personal commitments I couldn't back out of, and this constant need to keep going. I told myself, "Just push through, get it done, then you can relax." So, I could sleep at night properly because so many things were going to head, skipped meals, ignored the exhaustion creeping in, and convinced myself that taking a break only can change the situation. Then, one morning, I sat down at my desk, opened my laptop, and... nothing. My brain felt fried. The motivation? Gone. Even the simplest tasks felt impossible. Instead of working, I just sat there, staring at the screen, feeling completely drained. I wasn't being lazy—I was burnt out. And that wasn't enough, I was also dealing with a breakup at the time. Talk about bad timing, right? My mind was already overloaded with stress from work, and then, boom—emotional exhaustion on top of it. I kept pretending I was fine, telling myself, just focus on work, keep yourself busy. But the truth was, I wasn't fine. I was emotionally and physically drained and pretending I could handle everything. Heads-up: I couldn't. That moment hit me hard. I had been so focused on checking things off my list and distracting myself from my emotions that I didn't realize I was running on empty. And the worst part? I didn't even feel accomplished—I just felt exhausted and numb. That was my wake-up call.

I had to learn the hard way that being productive doesn't mean working yourself into the ground. And keeping busy isn't the same as healing. Pushing through exhaustion—whether it's from work, life, or heartbreak—doesn't make you stronger. It just makes you miserable. Real productivity comes from working intense, not just working supplementary. And sometimes, the smartest thing you can do is step back, take a breath, feel what you need to feel, and give yourself permission to rest. The key is to find a balance—staying productive without burning yourself out in the process. Here's how.

Stop Equating Productivity with Overworking- First things first— Stop thinking that the longer you work, the more productive you are—it's a trap. Being constantly busy doesn't mean you're achieving more; it just means you're exhausting yourself. I used to believe that working late nights and skipping breaks made me successful, but all it did was burn me out. Productivity isn't about doing more;

it's about doing better. A well-rested mind gets things done faster and with higher quality than an overworked one. Focus on what truly matters, set priorities, and work with intention. Success isn't measured by hours—it's measured by results. Work smarter, not longer, and watch how much more effective you become.

Listen to Your Energy, Not Just the Clock- Stop letting the clock dictate your day—start listening to your energy instead. Maybe you're someone who's sharpest in the morning, or perhaps you find your groove late at night. Pay attention to when you naturally feel the most focused and use that time for your most important tasks. I used to force myself to work at "normal" hours, ignoring that my brain wasn't fully awake yet. All it did was lead me straight to burnout. When you work with your energy, not against it, everything feels easier and more manageable. Trust your body'srhythm—it knows better than the clock ever will.

Take Breaks Without Feeling Guilty- If you think taking breaks is a waste of time, think again. So, stop feeling guilty about taking breaks—they're not a waste of time, they're a recharge for your brain. When you push through exhaustion, your focus drops, your creativity suffers, and everything takes longer. Instead of forcing yourself to power through, step away. Go for a walk, stretch, or just sit in silence for a few minutes. Real breaks help reset your mind and prevent burnout. And no, scrolling through social media doesn't count as a real break! Give yourself permission to pause, reset, and come back stronger. You'll get more done and feel better doing it.

Focus on Progress, Not Perfection- First of all no-one is perfect. If you think you are perfect then that's the biggest mistake. Because if you do mistake and learn from that mistake then there is the real growth. Perfectionism will drain you faster than hard work ever will. If you're always chasing the "perfect" outcome, you'll never feel satisfied—there will always be something to modify, fix, or improve. The truth is, perfection is an illusion, and waiting for it only holds you back. Instead, focus on progress and adapt. Small steps forward are better than standing still, look after every details. Done is always better than perfect. Learn, improve, and keep moving. Growth comes from action, not from obsessing over every flaw. Let go of perfection, and watch how much more you actually accomplish.

Make Time for What Recharges You- Stop treating the things you love as optional—they're not. I used to think that I wasn't working, I was wasting time. Every spare moment, I felt like I should be doing something productive, but eventually, I hit a wall. I felt drained, uninspired, and honestly, just unhappy. That's when I made a change. I started making time for things that actually made me feel good—morning walks, reading a book just for fun and guilt-free movie nights. At first, it felt weird, like I was slacking off. But you know what? I started feeling better. My energy came back, my creativity flowed again, and I realized that taking breaks wasn't a waste of time—it was fuel. Now, I make time for what recharges me, and I don't apologize for it. It's made all the difference. So go ahead, take that break, enjoy what makes you happy.You need it.

Check in with Yourself Regularly- I'll be honest, I didn't always check in with myself. After a breakup, I dove headfirst into work, thinking that if I stayed busy enough, I'd avoid dealing with the emotions that were piling up. But eventually, I realized I wasn't truly productive. I was just exhausted, mentally and physically, and nowhere near my best. I was burnt out, yet still trying to push through, thinking I had to keep going no matter what. That's when I decided to take a step back. I paused and asked myself, "Am I happy with what I'm doing? Am I even enjoying this anymore?" The answer was no. I was overwhelmed, emotionally drained, and running on empty. I had to reassess. So, I gave myself permission to slow down. I took breaks, spent time with my close friends, allowed myself to feel my emotions, and even gave myself the space to heal from the breakup. I realized that I didn't have to burn out to succeed. In fact, by respecting my limits and focusing on my mental well-being, I came back stronger. I was more focused, energized, and ready to take on my work with a clearer mind.

It wasn't easy, but it taught me that success doesn't have to come at the cost of your happiness or health. So, respecting your limits, and working with yourself, not against yourself, you can still achieve your goals and remember: you don't have to be broken to succeed—you just have to give yourself the time to identify, heal and grow.

Creating Sustainable Habits

CHAPTER TWENTY-SEVEN

THE 21/90 RULE: BUILDING LASTING HABITS

Sometimes, you start a good routine with enthusiasm, only to drop it within a few weeks? This happens since it takes time for habits to form and even longer for them to become life longing. The 21/90 Rule is a simple yet striking way of helping people shift from temporary changes to long-term habits: It takes 21 days to create a habit.

The Science of Behavioural Change: Turning that action into part of the routine takes 90 days. 90 days is not just any arbitrary number but is based on the psychology of building habits. When any action is repeated continuously for a period of 21 days, it becomes a set pattern in the mind. However, to automate it, that is, to be who we naturally are, requires a long-term investment in the direction of three months or 90 days.

Why Does the 21/90 Rule Work? Such a rule works because of the consistency rather than perfection; as the 21/90 rule says- it takes 21 days to form a habit and 90 days to make this action your lifestyle. Most people give up because they are expecting results instantly; the truth is that sustainable habits are built through small daily improvements, not overnight massive changes.

For instance, taking the example of introducing a reading habit in somebody: First 21 Days– Read for just 10 minutes daily religiously, no matter how 'engaged' the day is. Gradually extend the period of reading and make it part of the daily 'ritual' at a fixed time, e.g. at night before sleep. Thus, by day 90, reading will not feel like an effort—it will be second nature. End of the 90 days and reading will have become second nature.

What If You Miss a Day? One day is not the end of the road. Remember: the 2-Day Rule, which states "you shouldn't allow yourself to skip a habit for two consecutive days". Start again after one day without fear of losing momentum or motivation because you haven't. And that's the 21/90 Rule, and hence a game-changer if you really want to make substantive improvements in your life. It's not about size at the start but consistency for some time, letting transformation take place over time. It's about making behavior your identity; that's when change happens rather than trying to be.

CHAPTER TWENTY-EIGHT

HABIT STACKING FOR EFFICIENCY

Finding time to establish new habits can be a challenge in our busy lives. That's why habit stacking can be a powerful strategy. Instead of attempting to cram in a new habit into your schedule spontaneously, habit stacking is about attaching your new habit to a routine that already exists. That makes the new habit automatic as it is based on a behaviour you already make again and again. But based on the idea that our brain is wired on a pattern. This forms a "trigger-response system", making it easier to perform the new behaviour.

How habit stacking works? The concept: Stack a new habit to an existing one and do it so it's easy to remember and do as part of your daily routine. So, instead of forming a new habit on its own, you anchor it to something you reliably do already, which requires less willpower and makes you more likely to succeed. New actions paired with familiar ones result in automatic routinized behavior by the brain, which is always working to find its own patterns. The magic formula is simple: "After [existing habit], I will [new habit]", meaning that this new behavior slots seamlessly into your day. For example, "After brushing my teeth, I started to drink a glass of water." This approach of "Drinking water is the first thing in the morning that helps to hydrate my body and improve digestion", and you won't need to get motivated every time since it was already in practice. Eventually, stacked habits gain momentum, translating to major lifestyle changes over time with little work. The optimal way to use habit stacking is to begin with small, easy habits, establish mastery over them, and slowly add more once they've become second order. Then compound that with the fact that repeating the habit in association with an existing one helps to forge new neural pathways in the brain. When applied correctly, habit stacking allows you to create a new daily routine that boosts productivity and promotes gradual progress toward personal development without exhaustion. **Results After 30 Days:** By using a habit stack with things, I followed every day. I didn't have to 'find extra time' to improve myself—I simply added it to what I was already doing. Over time, these equally small habits compounded, improving my hydration, fitness, focus, and mental well-being without becoming a burden. My approach teaches us all how to turn daily actions into opportunities for self-growth by trying them to habits you'd like to cultivate.

THE SCIENCE OF BEHAVIOURAL CHANGE

Changing a behavior is not solely about willpower—it is a systematic approach that is influenced by psychological, neurobiological, and habit formation elements. Cue-response-reward loops oversee what we all do and don't do, associations that our brain forms between a behavior in a trigger situation and the outcome. In order to invoke sustainable change, we need to reconnect loops by changing our environment, frame of mind, and reinforcement. And the science behind changing your behavior is habit, motivation, and consistency working together to convert conscious acts into permanent routines.The Stages of Change model developed by James Prochaska includes **six phases** known as precontemplation, contemplation, preparation, action, maintenance, and relapse which researchers have extensively studied. People who want to quit smoking begin by rejecting the idea that smoking is harmful (**precontemplation**), before they start to think about how quitting could benefit them (**contemplation**). People might conduct research on nicotine patches (**preparation**) and then try to complete their first smoke-free day (**action**). As time passes, they focus on maintaining their results (**maintenance**) and learn strategies to regain their footing after (**relapsing**). People can move through behavior change with patience by understanding this model instead of becoming frustrated. Behavioral change depends heavily on neuroscience research. The brain's dopamine system manages motivation as it emits "feel-good" chemicals during achievement. Small wins keep us engaged because they matter so much in our progress. People who want to exercise regularly should begin with five-minute workouts rather than trying to complete daunting one-hour sessions. The brain releases dopamine neurotransmitters in response to small achievements which strengthens the habit and eases future continuation. Gradually the brain establishes new neural connections to want the fresh behavior until it becomes a normal daily routine.

Environmental design highlights the modification of surroundings in ways that place good habits within easy access and set major limits to bad habits. For example, for anyone wanting to eat a healthy diet, they should place those fruits and vegetables in plain, visible, and reachable places while keeping the junk food hidden away. This changes the choice one makes since the brain prefers to go for convenience than effort; this makes it easier to prefer healthier options. A student trying to cut screen time can also leave their phone in a different room while studying, thus removing the cue that makes them scroll through social media.

Accountability and social influence can also work as motivators for behavioural changes. Studies show that folks are more likely to stick to new habits when some other people are involved. Actual examples of this are workout partners: if one exercises alone, they may decide to skip it, but having that gym buddy at your side adds some responsibility to show up. The same goes for any public commitment: announcing to others on social media or letting a close friend know your goal of "I will wake up at 6 a.m. every day" will make you far more likely to see it through as the weight of disappointing people gives someone the motivation. Finally, self-identity is very important in any behavioural change. Instead of focusing on actions alone, a person should be more toward how one wants to identify himself or herself. For example, instead of saying to oneself, "I am trying to read more" one should say "I Am a Reader." The identity change strengthens commitment as people act as per their aspirations given how they see themselves.

Overcoming Setbacks &
Staying Motivated

CHAPTER THIRTY

LEARNING FROM FAILURES

I remember a time when failure hit me hard. I had put my heart and soul into a project, convinced it was going to work out exactly as I had planned. I spent countless hours perfecting every detail, sacrificing sleep, skipping meals, and pouring everything I had into it. But despite all my effort, it completely flopped. The outcome was nothing like I expected, and I felt like a complete failure. At first, I took it personally. I started questioning my abilities, wondering if I was even capable of success. The self-doubt crept in, and for a while, I wanted to give up. That experience taught me a valuable lesson: Failure is Feedback, Not Final —it's a chance to adjust. Think of failure as a message, not a label. When something doesn't work out, it's not the universe telling you that you're not good enough—it's simply an opportunity to learn. Maybe your approach wasn't right, maybe the timing was off, or maybe you needed more preparation. But none of those things mean you should give up. The only real failure is refusing to try again. I've personally had moments where I felt completely defeated. Whether it was a project that didn't take off, a job I didn't get, or a personal goal that fell apart, I used to take failure personally. But once I shifted my mindset, I realized that every setback was giving me valuable insight. Instead of seeing it as the end, I started asking myself, what can I take from this? That change in perspective made all the difference.

Analysing the Root Cause- One of the biggest mistakes we make is moving on from failure too quickly without really understanding why it happened. Instead of brushing it off, take the time to reflect. Ask yourself: What went wrong? What could I have done differently? What can I learn from this? Sometimes, failures happen because of things outside our control. But other times, they reveal areas we need to improve. The key is not to dwell on failure emotionally but to analyze it logically. If you failed an exam, was it because you didn't study enough or because you didn't understand the material? If a business idea flopped, was it due to lack of marketing, poor timing, or the wrong audience? Once you understand *why* something didn't work, you're in a much better position to succeed next time.

Building Resilience Through Small Wins- The best way to bounce back from failure is to focus on small victories. Instead of expecting overnight success, start by setting small, achievable goals. Each win—even a minor one—builds confidence and resilience. If you failed at something big, break it down into smaller steps and tackle them one at a time. I remember a time when I felt completely stuck after a major setback. Instead of trying to fix everything at once, I started focusing on small improvements—learning new skills, taking things step by step, and celebrating little achievements along the way. Over time, those small wins added up, and I found myself more confident and prepared for bigger challenges. If you ever feel like failure is the end of the road, just look at of the most successful people in history: Thomas Edison failed over 1,000 times before successfully inventing the lightbulb. When asked about it, he famously said, "I have not failed. I've just found 1,000 ways that won't work." Then "Walt Disney was fired from a newspaper for "lacking imagination" before he built one of the most successful entertainment companies in history."

Ultimate Views: Turning Failures into Firewood- So, if you're facing failure right now, know this—you're not alone, and this moment doesn't define you. And instead of dwelling on the pain, we grow, we evolve, and we come back stronger. What matters is what you do next. Learn from it, every setback carries a lesson, and those lessons are what ultimately lead to success. Because one day, you'll look back at this failure and realize it was the lesson that led you to success. Because at the end of the day, failure is never the end of the story—it's just the beginning of a new chapter.

THE ROLE OF SELF-REFLECTION IN GROWTH

When I felt completely stuck. I had put so much effort into everything—a project, a relationship, a personal goal—only to watch it fall apart. It felt like all my hard work had been for nothing. At first, I did what most people do—I blamed external factors, felt frustrated, and questioned whether I was even capable of success. But then, I decided to try something different: I started reflecting instead of reacting. One day I grabbed my laptop and started writing everything down—what went wrong, what I could have done better, and what lessons I could take from the experience. Instead of seeing the failure as an end, I started to break it down like a puzzle, looking for puzzle blocks on how I could improve. One major realization hit me: I was repeating patterns without even realizing it. I noticed that I would take on too much at once, and then feel disappointed when things didn't go as I planned. That pattern showed up in my work, in my personal life, and even in relationships. I wouldn't have seen it if I hadn't taken the time to note. The shift happened when I stopped seeing failure as something negative and started using it as feedback. I applied this to a breakup I had gone through as well. Instead of dwelling on the pain and blaming myself, I asked:

What did I do right in that relationship? – I gave my best, I was supportive, I was loyal, I was caring, as well as am the romantic one obviously and I was honest.

What I have done differently which affected my relationship? –Neglected my own boundaries, not taking care of myself much, not focusing on my career, I was too much into fix things that I forget to prioritized myself, I am not making him to realized his own mistake because I was afraid that I will lose him so whatever mistake he was doing am saying sorry and that the most foolish thing I had done.

What will I change next time? – I will prioritize clear communication, recognize when to walk away, and not lose myself in someone else.

This process didn't just help me heal—it helped me grow. The same approach applied to my professional setbacks. I started keeping a "Lessons Learned Log", tracking my mistakes and what they taught me. Over time, I noticed patterns in my decision-making, and instead of repeating the same mistakes, I adapted. Every time something doesn't go as per planned, I don't see it as failure—I see it as a lesson. Self-reflection has helped me move forward with more clarity and confidence. And the best part? When I look back at those past struggles, I realize they weren't the end of my journey—they were the stepping blocks to something better. Now you must be thinking how I find myself or how am I self-identified myself. Here are the simple things you can also follow:

The Power of Journaling- One of the most effective tools for self-reflection is **journaling**. Writing down your thoughts, feelings, failures, and lessons learned helps us process emotions and gain clarity. Sometimes, when things go wrong, our minds feel cluttered with frustration, regret, and self-doubt. But when we put those thoughts on paper, we can see them more objectively. I faced when I was struggling with self-doubt after a big setback. Instead of letting those negative thoughts consume me, I started writing them down—what I was feeling, what happened, and what I could take away from the experience. Journaling helped me shift my perspective. I realized that writing things down made me more aware of my emotions, my mistakes, and the steps I needed to take to improve. You don't have to be a writer to journal—just be honest with yourself. Whether you write a few sentences a day or a full page once a week, putting your thoughts into words will help you understand yourself better and track your growth over time.

Asking the Right Questions- Self-reflection isn't just about looking back—it's about asking the right questions. Instead of dwelling on Why did this happen to me? shift your mindset to questions that will actually help you grow: What did I do right? – Even in failure, there's always something you did well. Recognizing your strengths helps you build confidence. What could I have done differently? – This isn't about beating yourself up, but about seeing where adjustments can be made. What will I change next time? – Growth comes from learning, adapting, and doing things differently in the future. When we ask these types of questions, we stop blaming circumstances and start taking responsibility for our actions. That's when real change happens.

Growth vs. Fixed Mindset- The way we see failure and setbacks plays a huge role in our personal growth. If you have a fixed mindset, you might believe that intelligence, skills, and success are set in stone—that if you fail at something, it means you're not good enough. But if you develop a growth mindset, you understand that abilities can be improved with effort, and failures are just stepping stones to success. People with a growth mindset don't see setbacks as roadblocks; they see them as learning experiences. Instead of saying, I'm not good at this, they say, I'm not good at this yet, but I can learn. This small shift in mindset can make all the difference in how you approach challenges.

Creating a Personal "Lessons Learned" Log- One of the best ways to track your growth is by keeping a "Lessons Learned Log". This is a simple way to record past failures, the lessons you took from them, and the strategies you used to overcome them. Over time, this log becomes a personal blueprint for success—it shows you how far you've come and serves as a reminder that setbacks don't define you. "Write down a challenge or failure you faced- Be specific about what happened.", "List what you learned from the experience. What insights did you gain?", "Describe how you overcame it. What changes did you make? and what strategies worked for you?", "Reflect on how it has helped you grow. How did the experience shape you for the better?" Looking back at this log will remind you that failure is never the end—it's part of the process. The more you lcarn from your experiences, the stronger and wiser you become. So, take a step back, look at your journey so far, and ask yourself: What have I learned? How have I grown? And what will I do differently moving forward? The answers to these questions will shape your future.

CHAPTER THIRTY-TWO

KEEPING YOUR MOTIVATION HIGH

How I Keep My Motivation High – My Real-Life Experience: Motivation isn't something that magically stays with us every day. There was a time when I lost all motivation. Some days, I feel unstoppable, and other days, even the simplest tasks feel impossible. That's normal. I had started something with so much excitement—whether it was a project, a fitness goal, or even a relationship—but somewhere along the way, the fire faded. I found myself procrastinating, feeling stuck, and questioning if I should even continue or not. One of my biggest turning points was when I started writing. At first, I was filled with ideas and passion, but as time went on, self-doubt crept in. I kept thinking, what if no one reads this? What if it's not good enough? That negative mindset made it hard to stay consistent. But the key is knowing how to reignite your motivation when it starts to fade. It's not about forcing yourself to push through exhaustion—it's about finding ways to stay inspired, energized, and connected to your goals.

Reconnecting with My "Why"

As most of the time motivation fades away, we forget why we started in the first place. When things get tough, its easy to lose sight of the bigger picture. Then I had to pause and ask myself, 'Why did I start this in the first place? 'what's the deeper reason behind my goals', 'How I will feel once I achieve it? 'Writing wasn't just about putting words on a page—it was my way of expressing myself, sharing my journey, and maybe even helping someone who felt the same way I did. Once I reminded myself of that purpose, it reignited my motivation. Your "why" is what completes you. If you're struggling to stay motivated, remind yourself of the purpose behind your actions. Write it down. Say it out loud. Keep it visible. When your reason is strong enough, you'll find a way to keep going, even on the hard days.

Breaking It Down into Small Wins: One of the biggest motivation killers is feeling overwhelmed. When your goal seems too big, your brain automatically wants to procrastinate. Another thing that helped me was breaking my big goals into smaller steps. Start small, stay consistent, and celebrate progress along the way. Instead of telling myself, "One day I will publish a book", I focused on writing my daily journal of superproductive every day, I focused on making small progress daily. Little by little, those small wins-built momentum and momentum is what keeps motivation alive.

Fixing My Environment: Your environment has a huge impact on your motivation. If you're constantly around negative people who don't support your goals, it's going to drain your energy. I started following people who inspired me instead of those who made me doubt myself. I spent more time around people who encouraged me. And if you are surrounded by negative environment no need to worry, create your own space and surround by yourself, no need to seek for validation from other. Because you know your purpose, when something new you will start maybe that time no one will agree with you. But when they will see your worth, they will try to follow the same path- it's funny but that's the reality. I have seen some people like this, maybe you have also seen. That's why it's important to choose your environment wisely. Stay with people who inspire and uplift you, who motivates you, not discourages you. Create habits that set you up for success. If you want to stay motivated, be intentional about who and what you allow into your space. Energy is contagious—so make sure you're surrounded by the right kind.

I've learned the hard way that not everyone who's drawn to my energy is meant to stay in my life. Because of my naturally positivity and lively nature, I tend to attract people, and I've always welcomed them with an open heart out of kindness. But over time, I noticed a pattern—while they walked away feeling inspired, happy, and confident. I end up feeling completely drained, dull and empty. It took me a while to understand that energy is precious, and not everyone deserves access to it: you have to be mindful of who you allow into your space. The right people will pour into you just as much as you pour into them, while the wrong ones will take and leave you running on empty. Choose wisely.

Balancing Work and Rest: If you consume pleased that makes you doubt yourself, your confidence will take a hit. There were days when I forced myself to work even when I felt mentally exhausted. But I learned that pushing too much only led to burnout. Real motivation comes from balance-knowing when to push and when to rest. So, I started listening to my body. Some days, instead of work, I allowed myself to take a break and rest. It isn't a waste of time; it's necessary for long-term success- a good nap, watch a movie, or just do nothing. Ironically, the more I respected my need for rest, the more productive I became. Even I changed my workspace to make it more comfortable and motivating. So, prioritize rest, recharge, and come back stronger otherwise your motivation will suffer

Using Affirmations and Visualization: Your mind is powerful. If you constantly thinking negative your brain will capture negativity only. That's why positive self-talk and visualization are so important. I also started changing my self-talk. Instead of saying, *I'm not good enough,* I started saying, I'm improving every day, and my words matter. I also visualized the feeling of completing my work, the impact it could have, and how proud I would feel. Slowly, my mindset shifted.

Visualization: Close your eyes and imagine yourself achieving your goal. Picture every detail—how it feels, what it looks like, the sense of accomplishment. Your brain doesn't know the difference between real and imagined experiences, so visualizing success makes it feel more achievable. For example- If you are planning to buy a luxury car, don't think one day you will buy that car, just go to the details- Imagine you are opening the car's door, then you are sitting inside the car and driving. Every minor detail you have to think

Affirmations: Speak to yourself with confidence. Instead of saying, *I hope I can do this,* say, *I am capable, I am strong, and I will succeed.* The way you talk to yourself shapes your reality.

The Lesson? Motivation Isn't Magic—It's a Choice: Motivation isn't something you wake up with every day—it's something you build through habits, mindset, and consistency. I realized that motivation doesn't just appear—it's something we create by how we think, how we set up our goals, and how we take care of ourselves. Some days, I still struggle, but now I know what to do when that happens. If you ever feel like giving up, pause-reconnecting with your "why,", setting realistic goals, surrounding yourself with the right energy, prioritizing rest, and using positive reinforcement, with kindness. Motivation isn't about feeling inspired 24/7, the fire isn't gone yet—it just needs a little spark to come back. And trust me, you'll find that spark again.

The 1% Rule: Continuous Improvement

CHAPTER THIRTY-THREE

SMALL DAILY IMPROVEMENTS FOR MASSIVE RESULTS

When we think of success, we often imagine big, life-changing moments—the huge promotions, the dramatic weight loss transformations, or the overnight success stories. Fact? Real success comes from small, daily improvements. I used to believe that success required huge, dramatic efforts. I thought I had to work hard for hours to be successful, work out intensely, or completely change my habits overnight to see progress. But every time I tried that, I burned out quickly and ended up right back where I started. It was frustrating. Then, I started focusing on small daily improvements instead of overwhelming myself with big goals. And let me tell you—this mindset changed everything. The tiny things you do every day might not seem like much at first, but over time, they create massive results.

My Writing Journey: One Paragraph at a Time- When I first started writing, I never thought of I will write an entire book that I needed to complete entire chapters in one sitting. Rather than that I used to right every day for 1hr. That's it. Even if it was a messy draft, even if it wasn't perfect—I just had to show up and write. At first, it didn't feel like much. But after a week, those small paragraphs turned into pages. After a month, I had multiple chapters. And before I knew it, I had a solid draft. The lesson? Big progress happens when you commit to small, consistent actions. Take a look, Power of Compounding- think of it like saving money. If you invest a little every day, it might not feel significant, but over time, thanks to compounding, that small amount turns into something huge. The same principle applies to personal growth, fitness, learning, and even relationships. Reading just 10 pages of a book every day adds up to 3,650 pages in a year—that's around 10–15 books! Doing 10 push-ups a day might seem small, but in a year, that's 3,650 push-ups—a huge impact on your strength and fitness. Spending just 5 minutes daily learning a new skill means you'll have invested 30 hours in that skill by the end of the year—and that's enough to become significantly better. Small efforts don't stay small. They grow.

From doing nothing to doing something- I've always admired people who could hit the gym consistently. But every time I tried, I would push too hard, get exhausted, and quit after a few weeks. It felt impossible to keep up. So instead of forcing myself into an intense routine, I decided to start. I committed to just 5 minutes of movement every day. So, some days, it was a short walk. Other days, it was a few stretches. Eventually, I started doing short workouts. It felt easy at first, but those small sessions built the habit of movement. Before I realized it, I was working out four to five times a week without forcing myself. One of the biggest mistakes people make is believing they have to be picture-perfect to see results. What's actually matters is consistency in everything. If you're working on a project, you don't need to complete it in one go—doing a little bit every day will eventually get it done. True growth doesn't come from a single perfect effort—it comes from the small, consistent steps you take every day. That's what really makes a difference.

The 1% Mindset Shift: Learning and Growth- I used to think that if I couldn't dedicate hours to learning something new, there was no point in even trying. But then I shifted my approach. The idea of changing your life can feel overwhelming. Instead of trying to master something overnight, I asked myself: "How can I improve just 1% today?" So, I started reading 10 pages a day instead of trying to finish an entire book in one sitting. I spent a few minutes journaling to track my progress, rather than trying to make big life changes all at once. I started learning new things related to my field to finished my course. Instead of changing your entire diet overnight, start by adding one healthy meal a day. If you improve by just 1% daily, by the end of a year, you'll be 37 times better than when you started. That's the power of small daily improvements.

Look at your surroundings everyone is going to Ed Sheeran concert- Ed Sheeran didn't start out as the singer we know today. In the beginning, he performed at small gigs, practiced every day, and kept improving. Over time, that daily commitment turned him into a global superstar. Then, everyone buying something from Amazon- Jeff Bezos started Amazon from a garage, selling books online. He didn't build a billion-dollar company overnight. He focused on small improvements—one product, one customer, one decision at a time—until Amazon became what it is today. Over time, those tiny efforts added up. I became more knowledgeable, more confident, and more capable.

Final thought- Success doesn't come from one giant effort—it comes from the tiny choices you make daily. So, instead of waiting for the "perfect" time or overwhelming yourself with huge goals, just focus on getting 1% better every day. I've experienced this in my own life too. I used to feel overwhelmed whenever I had a big goal—whether it was writing, professional, fitness, or personal growth. But once I stopped aiming for massive leaps and focused on daily progress, everything changed. And before you know it, those tiny steps will lead to something massive

"One small habit. One small action. One small improvement."

Because small daily improvements turn into massive results—I've seen it happen in my own life. And trust me, if I can do it, so can you.

THE KAIZEN APPROACH TO PERSONAL GROWTH

Kaizen is a Japanese philosophy that means "continuous improvement." It's the idea that instead of chasing perfection or massive change overnight, you focus on small, consistent improvements every day. The beauty of Kaizen is that it works in every area of life—your career, habits, relationships, health, and even your mindset. It teaches us that tiny, intentional changes add up over time, leading to massive results without overwhelming us.

How Kaizen Transformed My Life- For the longest time, I wanted to be productive, I had to completely overhaul my routine. If I wanted to be fit, I had to follow an intense workout plan. If I wanted to be a better writer, I had to write thousands of words a day. But every time I tried to change everything at once, I burned out fast. I would start strong, feel overwhelmed, and eventually quit. That's when I discovered Kaizen—the power of small, continuous improvements.

Kaizen in Habits- Instead of trying to read an entire book in a day, read 5 pages every night before bed. Want to get fit? Start with just 5 minutes of exercise daily instead of forcing an hour-long workout. Struggling to wake up early? Try waking up 5 minutes earlier each day instead of making a drastic jump.

Kaizen in Work & Productivity- Improve your skills by learning one new thing every day rather than waiting for the "perfect time" to start. If a task feels overwhelming, break it down into smaller, manageable steps and tackle them one at a time. Instead of multitasking and feeling scattered, focus on one small improvement—like organizing your workspace for better efficiency.

Kaizen in Relationships- Want to strengthen your relationships? Express appreciation daily, even if it's just a simple "thank you" or a kind message. Instead of trying to change everything about your communication style overnight, focus on one small improvement, like listening more in conversations. If you're working on trust or connection, be consistent with small efforts—showing up, being honest, and making time for quality moments, don't give up easily and don't make assumption by overthinking, make it clear then and there only. By understanding each other things go smoothly, but building up a relationship and understand each other took a lot of time, for few its easy to go. So breaking up is not only the solution.

Kaizen in Self-Development- Instead of feeling overwhelmed by self-improvement books, take **one** key lesson from each and apply it before moving to the next. Want to build confidence? Start by practicing small acts of courage, like speaking up in a meeting or trying something new. Work on your mindset by writing down one positive thing daily instead of forcing yourself to be "positive all the time.

Kaizen in My Writing Journey: I always dreamed of writing a book, but I kept postponing it. I thought I needed the perfect idea, the perfect outline, and long hours of uninterrupted writing to make it happen. One day, I decided to apply Kaizen. Instead of overwhelming myself with unrealistic goals, I told myself, "As am writing journal every day for 1hr, why can't I write a book now? Afterall, I wrote so many pages." At first, it felt insignificant. But as the days passed, 1 hr turned into a few pages, then chapters. Slowly but surely, my book started coming to life. What I learned? Small progress is still progress. And over time, small daily efforts lead to something big. These small changes felt easy, but they compounded over time and made a huge impact on my mindset and habits.

Final Takeaway: Kaizen isn't about just doing more—it's about doing something than nothing and making moves to improve efficiency. So, if you feel stuck or overwhelmed Just ask yourself: What's one tiny thing I can do today to get better? The power of Kaizen is in its simplicity, you just need to focus on your small moves. Kaizen teaches us is that failure isn't a bad thing—it's a chance to improve. Instead of seeing setbacks as "that you're not good enough", see them as opportunities to learn and adjust.

CHAPTER THIRTY-FIVE

CREATING A LONG-TERM PRODUCTIVITY PLAN

How I Built a Long-Term Productivity Plan (and Navigated a Major Life Change) Previously, I thought productivity meant pushing through no matter what—working harder, forcing routines, and sticking to a rigid plan. Later I understood that real productivity is about adaptability, consistency, and knowing when to pivot. One of the biggest shifts in my life happened when I decided to change my educational stream, and that experience taught me the true power of a long-term productivity plan.

Setting Micro-Goals for Lasting Change- Changing my educational path wasn't easy. At first, I felt lost and overwhelmed. I had to learn new subjects, adjust to a different way of thinking, and, honestly, I questioned if I had made the right decision. Instead of letting the fear of the unknown hold me back, I broke everything down into small, manageable steps. I started by learning the basics instead of diving straight into advanced concepts. I committed to studying just 30 minutes a day, rather than overwhelming myself with long study sessions. I focused on progress, not perfection. Even if I didn't grasp everything right away, I reminded myself that I was improving bit by bit. Over time, those small efforts added up, and before I knew it, I became confident in my new field.

Adjusting & Adapting- When I first switched streams, I thought I had to study the way others did. I tried following traditional study techniques, but they didn't work for me. I realized that forcing myself into someone else's strategy was setting me up for failure. So, I adjusted my approach: Instead of reading textbooks for hours, I started using video lessons and real-world applications to understand concepts faster. Instead of memorizing, I focused on practical learning—applying knowledge through small projects and discussions. Instead of pressuring myself to learn everything at once, I focused on masteringone topic at a time. This flexible approach made studying more effective and less stressful.

Building a Lifestyle of Growth- At first, changing my educational stream felt like starting from zero, but looking back, I realize it was a step toward continuous growth. Now, I apply this growth mindset to everything: If I struggle with something new, I remind myself it's part of the process. If a strategy isn't working, I adjust instead of quitting. If I feel behind, I focus on small wins instead of comparing myself to others.

The Biggest Lesson? Progress Beats Perfection. Changing my educational stream taught me that productivity isn't about sticking to a rigid plan—it's about being flexible, learning as you go, and trusting the process. If you're feeling stuck, remember: You don't have to have it all figured out today. Just take small steps, adjust as needed, and keep moving forward. One day, you'll look back and realize how far you've come.

Start your journey with Simple yet powerful habits:

Rise Early: As I woke up early, it gave me quiet time to plan my personal growth and mindset for the day.

AM Mindfulness + Journaling: Every morning I wrote my thoughts and goals down on paper; this ensured my intentions were clear and I was moving forward.

Exercise: Implementing exercises into my plan has really helped to increase my energy, and clear my mind.

Nutrition: A balanced consumption of food has always played a pivotal role when it comes down to fuelling my body and mind for extensive productivity.

Reading all the time: Reading books and learning new subjects helped me to stay mentally active and adaptable.

Self-Reflection: Following my progress periodically gave me a chance to address shortcomings and reward accomplishments.

Gratitude Practice: Looking at the brighter sides of my life helped me build mental toughness.

Planning: Having clearly defined short term and long-term goals gave me something to work towards.

Productivity: Organizing my activities in order of importance and reducing the number of interruptions to my work improved my productivity.

Affirmations: Engaging in positive self-talk fuelled my confidence and self-esteem.

Active Community Participation: Getting involved in the community made me feel better about myself and gave me a reason to live.

Adaptability: Changing my mindset and being accepting toward new situations helped me find solutions to problems.

Self-Care: Doing activities which made me feel good has always kept me in a good mental and physical state so I can take good care of myself.

Digital Detox: Setting limitations on how much time I spend in front of screens helped me greatly with staying focused instead of worrying about everything.

Maintaining a Tidy Workspace: Making sure that my working area is clean and organized helped me focus more, thus increasing my work productivity.

Sleeping Patterns: By getting the valuable sleep I needed, my body and mind was fully prepared for what the next day may bring.

Unhealthy Dealings: Keeping meaningful relationships gave me the chance to obtain a broader point of view as well as support.

Mindfulness and Meditation: Engaging in mindfulness practices focused my attention and helped me de-stress.

Creative Expression: Partaking in creative activities enhanced my innovation and problem-solving abilities.

Finances: Looking after my financial responsibilities gave me less stress and more security.

Celebrating Wins: Seeing my hard work pay off, no matter how small, gave the motivation needed to keep working.